Jim Maynard's

Y0-BEO-845

POCKET ASTROLOGER®
2012

This year's cover artist is Pat Brown. Pat is an astrologer, columnist, lecturer, and artist. Pat has been a regular on guest talk shows and has appeared on national television. She did this painting originally for the 1977 Celestial Calendars.

The zodiac illustrations are from Digital Vision Ltd.

A wall calendar version of the **Pocket Astrologer**® is available as the **Celestial Influences**®, 48 pages, unfolding to 12 x 18 inches, with color illustrations for $12⁹⁵. **Celestial Guide**® is a week-at-a-glance engagement calendar, 5⅜ x 8½ inches, 176 pages, b&w illustrations, and available with either a plastic spiral binding for $11⁹⁵ or as 7-hole punched, loose pages for a 3-, 5-, or 7-ring binder, also $11⁹⁵. **Astrologer's Datebook**® is a smaller version of Celestial Guide®, 4¼ x 6¾ inches, with a sewn binding for $8⁹⁵. See page 64 or www.QuicksilverProductions.com for more information.

Printed in China

Published by QUICKSILVER PRODUCTIONS
P. O. Box 340, Ashland, Oregon 97520 U.S.A.

Planetary Motions

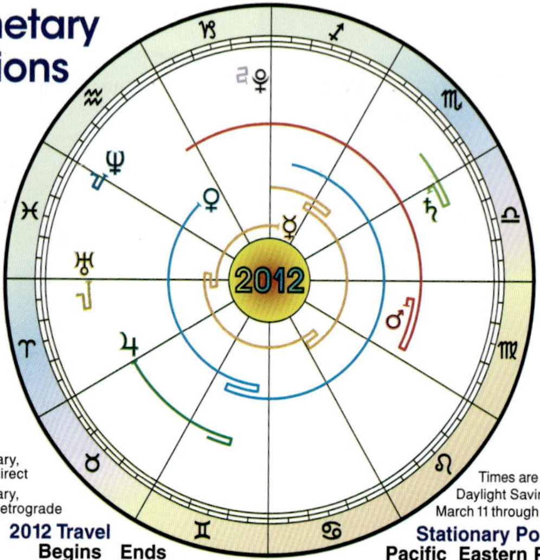

SD = Stationary, going Direct
SR = Stationary, going Retrograde

Times are corrected for Daylight Saving Time from March 11 through November 4.

Planet	2012 Travel Begins	Ends	Stationary Points		Pacific	Eastern	Position
Mercury ☿	20♐30	29♐52	SR	March 12	0:49a	3:49a	6♈49
			SD	April 4	3:11a	6:11a	23♓51
			SR	July 14	7:16p	10:16p	12♌33
			SD	August 7/8	10:40p	1:40a	1♌26
			SR	November 6	3:04p	6:04p	4♐18
			SD	November 26	2:48p	5:48p	18♏10
Venus ♀	14♒26	19♐08	SR	May 15	7:33a	10:33a	23♊59
			SD	June 27	8:07a	11:07a	7♊29
Mars ♂	20♍14	4♒17	SR	January 23	4:54p	7:54p	23♍06
			SD	April 13	8:53p	11:53p	3♍41
Jupiter ♃	0♉26	7♊49℞	SR	October 4	6:18a	9:18a	16♊23
Saturn ♄	28♎19	9♏30	SR	February 7	6:03a	9:03a	29♎30
			SD	June 25	1:01a	4:01a	22♎46
Uranus ♅	0♈51	4♈45	SR	July 13	2:49a	5:49a	8♈32
			SD	December 13	4:02a	7:02a	4♈37
Neptune ♆	28♒54	1♓03	SR	June 4	2:05p	5:05p	3♓09
			SD	November 10/11	11:53p	2:53a	0♓22
Pluto ♇	7♑20	9♑18	SR	April 10	9:21a	12:21p	9♑34
			SD	Sept. 17/18	10:05p	1:05a	6♑57

CONTENTS

Planets in Morning or Evening Twilight

	Morning	Evening
Mercury ☿	January 1 – January 24 March 29 – May 20 August 6 – September 1 Nov. 24 – December 31	February 19 – March 14 June 4 – July 21 Sept. 22 – Nov. 12
Venus ♀	June 13 – December 31	January 1 – May 30
Mars ♂	January 1 – March 3	March 3 – December 31
Jupiter ♃	May 28 – December 3	January 1 – April 29 December 3 – Dec. 31
Saturn ♄	January 1 – April 15 November 12 – Dec. 31	April 15 – October 8

2012 Eclipses & Transit of Venus

I. Annular Eclipse of the Sun, May 20–21, 0♊21. An annular eclipse has a narrow ring of the Sun visible beyond the dark mask of the Moon. Annular phase will be visible on the Chinese coast, the south of Japan, and west U.S. and Canada. Tokyo will be on the central path. The maximum will occur in the N. Pacific, south of the Aleutian islands, and end in the west U.S.

The partial eclipse will be visible over most of Asia, Russia, and northwest North America. This eclipse has a very wide path and long durations. The Sun will not be darkened as much as in shorter-lasting eclipses.

Eclipse beginning; first contact with Earth	May 20, 20:56.1 GMT
Beginning of southern limit of penumbra	21:42.4 GMT
Beginning of southern limit of umbra	22:07.4 GMT
Beginning of center line; central eclipse begins	22:09.0 GMT
Beginning of northern limit of umbra	22:10.6 GMT
Central eclipse at local apparent noon	23:59.1 GMT
End of northern limit of umbra	May 21, 01:34.8 GMT
End of center line; central eclipse ends	01:36.4 GMT
End of southern limit of umbra	01:38.0 GMT
End of southern limit of penumbra	02:03.1 GMT
Eclipse ends; last contact with Earth	02:49.3 GMT

II. Partial Eclipse of the Moon, June 4, 14♐14. The Moon passes partially into the northern umbral shadow. The portion of the moon within the penumbral shadow will be significantly dimmed. The portion in the umbral shadow will be much dimmer with a reddish hue. This eclipse is visible from the Americas, the Pacific, eastern Asia, Australia and Antarctica.

Moon enters penumbra	08:46.5 GMT
Beginning of umbra	09:59.3 GMT
Middle of eclipse	11:03.2 GMT
End of umbra	12:07.0 GMT
Moon leaves penumbra	13:19.9 GMT

2012 Most Visible Meteor Showers

April 21–22 *April Lyrids* at 15 meteors/hour
August 12–13 *Perseids* at 40 meteors/hour
October 21–22 *Orionids* at 30 meteors/hour
November 16–17 *Leonids* at 15 meteors/hour
December 13 ±2 days *Geminids* at 85 meteors/hour

Hourly rates are for a rural, moonless sky.
"Most Visible" meteor showers are those occurring within 6 days of a New Moon.

Chinese Year of the Elder, Water, Dragon: Lunar Year 4710

In 2012 the Chinese New Year begins January 23rd in the U.S.

III. Transit of Venus, June 5–6, 15Ⅱ45. This entire transit of Venus over the Sun will be visible in northwest N. America, Hawaii, western Pacific, north Asia, Japan, Korea, east China, Philippines, New Zealand, and eastern Australia. Transit is still in progress at sunset for most of North America, Caribbean, and northwest S. America. The transit is already in progress at sunrise for central Asia, Middle East, Europe, and eastern Africa.

Ingress, exterior contact . . . . June 5, 22:09.7 GMT
Ingress, interior contact . . . . 22:27.5 GMT
Least angular distance . . . . June 6, 01:29.6 GMT
Egress, interior contact . . . . 04:31.7 GMT
Egress, exterior contact . . . . 04:49.5 GMT

IV. Total Eclipse of the Sun, November 13–14, 21♏57. The total phase will only be visible in northern Australia and the South Pacific. Only the beginning of the eclipse occurs over land. The partial phase will be visible over much of Australia, all of New Zealand, and the South Pacific.

Eclipse begins; first contact with Earth . . . . 19:37.9 GMT
Beginning of northern limit of penumbra . . . . 20:22.1 GMT
Beginning of northern limit of umbra . . . . 20:35.6 GMT
Beg. of center line; central eclipse begins . . . . 20:36.1 GMT
Beginning of southern limit of umbra . . . . 20:36.5 GMT
Beginning of southern limit of penumbra . . . . 21:32.1 GMT
Central eclipse at local apparent noon . . . . 22:18.0 GMT
End of southern limit of penumbra . . . . 22:51.3 GMT
End of southern limit of umbra . . . . 23:46.9 GMT
End of center line; central eclipse ends . . . . 23:47.4 GMT
End of northern limit of umbra . . . . 23:47.9 GMT
End of northern limit of penumbra . . . . 00:01.5 GMT
Eclipse ends; last contact with Earth . . . . 00:45.5 GMT

V. Penumbral Eclipse of the Moon, November 28, 6Ⅱ47. The northern parts of the moon will perceptibly dim as the moon passes through the Earth's penumbral shadow. This eclipse is visible in Europe, eastern Africa, Asia, Australia, the Pacific Ocean, and most of North America.

Moon enters penumbra . . . . 12:12.6 GMT
Middle of eclipse . . . . 14:33.0 GMT
Moon leaves penumbra . . . . 16:53.3 GMT

Signs of the Zodiac

♈ **Aries**, the first sign of the zodiac, is the emergence of the sprouting seed, the point of all beginnings. Aries is the outrushing force, sound and fury, primitive self-expression, the joy of being. Its forcefulness is like the ram which lowers its head and blindly charges. The Aries influence gives an adventurous, pioneering spirit, courage, and a blunt and direct manner. The forcefulness of Aries is so strong that restrictions cannot be endured. Aries people are forever moving to new projects, seldom completing the old ones. An Aries person inhibited by daily routine and a sedentary life is likely to eventually explode. The "me first" attitude of Aries can go to the extremes of selfishness, crudeness, egotistical attitudes, and foolhardiness if it's not tempered by sensitivity to others and strong guiding ideals.

♉ **Taurus** combines the concentrated nature of a fixed sign with the practicality of earth. Taurus people, being ruled by Venus, love beauty and are often quite charming. They're very affectionate, but their strong need for security sometimes lets their affectionate nature become possessive. Taurus people are strongly rooted in their opinions and can be stubborn and don't like to be contradicted. They *can* change but don't expect it to happen more than once! They're particularly patient and often reliable and practical, if their laziness and inertia don't get the better of them. Taurus people have incredible endurance and often have an excellent business sense. They crave luxury, art, and good food.

♊ **Gemini** is a mutable air sign. Some people think Gemini has neither positive nor negative polarity. This is the sign of the twins, Castor and Pollux, who are the two sides of one personality. In Gemini the restless intelligence of air combines with the adaptability of a mutable sign. Ruled by Mercury, Gemini emphasizes communication. Geminis are versatile, logical, sometimes witty, inquisitive, and spontaneous. They also tend to be nervous, restless, superficial, and inconsistent. The metal of Gemini is Quicksilver, or Mercury, which has no shape of its own. Try to hold it! It flows through your fingers as does the elusive Gemini.

♋ **Cancer**, with the unstable, emotional nature of water expressed in the cardinal mode, becomes restless. However, the self-repressive nature tends to keep this energy below the surface, with Cancers pursuing rather definite goals in secretive or unconscious ways. Much like their symbol, the crab, Cancers can appear hard and insensitive on the outside, yet they are soft and vulnerable on the inside, at times even overly sensitive and easily hurt. Like the crab, Cancers are evasive, always side-stepping, preferring not to confront anything too directly. They tend to hide within their shells and will often resist your prying into their secret lives.

Cancer is ruled by the Moon, giving it a flowing, emotional nature and an abundantly fertile imagination. Cancers are sensitive, cautious, kind, sympathetic, protective, shrewd, and resourceful. However, their moody emotionalism can, at times, get out of hand.

♌ **Leo** combines the burning enthusiasm of fire with the powerful expression of its fixed nature. Leo is ruled by the strongest "planet," the Sun. Leos need to be the center of attention. They're creative, graceful, proud, dignified, determined, and dramatic. They are very generous, enthusiastic, expansive, and often good organizers. Their negative traits include being conceited, snobbish, intolerant, patronizing, dogmatic, and pompous. Leos need to feel the divine nobility of their existence. Then they can allow their warmheartedness to shine through and they can be tremendous sources of love and encouragement for others.

♍ **Virgo** is a practical earth sign, introverted like Taurus by its negative polarity, but enjoying the freedom and adaptability of its mutable nature. Virgo is addicted to practical, material objects but is not as possessive as Taurus. Virgo, like Gemini, is ruled by Mercury, but here the communicative nature of Mercury is used on a practical level. Virgos are discriminating, critical, analytical, meticulous, modest, and orderly. They can be worriers, overly fastidious, finicky, too critical, and too conventional. Virgo's intellect lacks breadth, but it's great at details and facts. They analyze everything, which is valuable in dealing with our bureaucratic modern society. Virgo desperately needs to work, to feel useful and to be of service to others.

♎ **Libra** is active and aggressive, but not in an obvious manner. This mode of expression combines with the flowing communicative and intelligent nature of air signs. Libra's energy is searching for balance. While Libra is considered to have a positive polarity (yang), it is ruled by negative (yin) Venus, the receptive planet of charm and beauty. Libras idolize harmony. Sometimes, fearful of discord, they become indecisive. They easily see the value of each point of view, often because they don't hold a definite opinion of their own. In their search for balance, Libras strive to show both sides. Libras can be frivolous, gullible, and flirtatious, but also diplomatic, idealistic, romantic, easygoing, and they have a refined appearance.

♏ **Scorpio**, a fixed sign, is true to its convictions, set in its ways. It's ruled by energetic Mars and by Pluto, the planet of intense desires. The negative polarity gives Scorpio a responsive nature, with much of its Martian forcefulness hidden from view. It's also a water sign, giving it an unstable, emotional nature with powerful feelings, emotions, and a strong sense of purpose. The dichotomy of its fixity and instability often leaves Scorpio at war with itself. Scorpios are very imaginative, subtle, and determined, but can also be resentful, stubborn, secretive, suspicious, and jealous. They're self-contained, may be self-centered, and have lots of stored energy ready to burst forth. Whatever Scorpios really want to achieve, they probably will. They have a great deal of personal magnetism and healing power.

♐ **Sagittarius** is the centaur shooting for great heights. Aspiration is their key. They aim high and they cover a lot of ground, even more than Gemini, their complement. They have the adaptability of a mutable sign, self-expressiveness of positive polarity, and the energy and enthusiasm of fire. Ruled by expansive Jupiter, they are travelers and philosophers. Sagittarians are freedom loving and need space. They're friendly, sincere, outgoing, versatile, dependable, open-minded, excitable, jovial, optimistic, and can also be irresponsible, tactless, capricious, arrogant, and dogmatic. But they can also be beautifully positive, encouraging people.

♑ **Capricorn**'s earthy, outgoing cardinality is applied on the practical level of everyday necessities. The sign's negative polarity gives Capricorns the ability to withdraw from the turbulence of the mainstream and to bide their time until the situation is ripe for their ambitions.

Capricorns are reliable, practical, ambitious, prudent, efficient, persistent and patient, and they have a good but dry sense of humor. Ruled by the contracting, concentrated energy of Saturn, they can also be cold and rigid, pessimistic, and intolerably conventional. Saturn rulership also makes time important in Capricorn's life. They're often slow to develop, requiring more time than others. At middle age they often seem to be at a plateau, not changing for decades, while their contemporaries age at a normal pace.

♒ **Aquarius**' outgoing, self-expressive positive polarity combines with the communicative nature of air. Intellectual Aquarians are disseminators of knowledge. With a fixed nature, they're unlikely to budge from their preconceived ideas but usually have a progressive outlook. They're original, inventive, friendly, independent, idealistic, and revolutionary, sometimes even straining to be unconventional. They're very loving, but this is more easily expressed in a detached concern for groups rather than individuals. Aquarians, ruled by Uranus, the erratic revolutionary, must have their freedom and close personal relationships are often too restrictive.

♓ **Pisces** is unstable, flowing water combining with the mutable ability to easily drift through change, making it the most fluid sign of the zodiac. The introverted nature of the negative polarity predominates. Pisces is the most sensitive of the signs with very strong and deep emotions. Pisceans are much too impressionable, too susceptible to outside influences and often need to escape. Ruled by the nebulous planet Neptune, they can be quite difficult to understand. It helps to remember that unworldly Pisceans operate on an intuitive level, often needing to retreat to maintain their equilibrium. They cannot be understood through logic, analysis or pressure. They can give vast amounts of compassion, are self-sacrificing, often kind, sympathetic, receptive, intuitive, and humble. However, they can also be indecisive, vague, secretive, careless, and not good at dealing with the physical world.

The Planets

Planets are the focal points of energy. They're indicators of specific, unique kinds of activity, but colored by the nature of the sign the planet is in. The sign most like the nature of a particular planet is said to be ruled by that planet. Positive (yang) planets are the Sun, Mars, Jupiter, Uranus, and Pluto. They activate, project, stimulate, and vitalize. Negative (yin) planets, the Moon, Venus, Saturn, and Neptune, are receptive, reactive, responsive, and protective. Mercury is a neutral planet which modifies, interprets, or communicates the energies of other planets in aspect to it.

☉ The **Sun** represents the will: the power urge, the vitalizing, life-giving force. It is the symbol of masculinity, paternity, authority, creative ability, ambition, pride, leadership, self-expression, determination, and confidence. The Sun creates, achieves, elevates, dominates, sustains, fortifies, promotes, and illuminates. It is the ruling planet of Leo, a sign of creativity and leadership. It is exalted in willful Aries, indicating that the Sun's individuality can be expressed in a powerful and pure form through Aries.

☽ The **Moon** rules all things of a watery nature. It rules the tides and rhythms of the body as well as the oceans.

The Moon represents the personality, the subconscious or subjective mind and our instinctual behavior. It is associated with instincts, habits, memory, imagination, receptivity, impressionability, the desire for fresh experiences, femininity, maternity, fertility, disposition, emotions, feelings, moods, sensitivity, intuition, sensation, and sympathy. The Moon is strongest in the nurturing sign of Cancer and weakest in unreceptive, unemotional Capricorn. The Moon is also powerful in Taurus and can be emotionally problematic in Scorpio.

☿ **Mercury** represents the mind—the link between spirit and matter, between soul and personality. Mercury symbolizes the power of communication and interpretation: intelligence, reasoning capacities and the ability to perceive relationships and gather facts. Mercurial qualities also include being adaptable, attentive, perceptive, clever, versatile, inconsistent, hypercritical, argumentative, sarcastic, cynical, excitable, impressionable, and nervous or prone to worry. Mercury narrates, talks, memorizes, debates, writes, argues, analyzes, studies, travels, sells, reflects, and expresses with the hands as well as the tongue.

Mercury is of neither positive nor negative polarity—neither masculine nor feminine. Mercury rules all communications and is associated with speaking and writing, educational capacities and manual skills.

Mercury is especially active in the versatile, talkative sign of Gemini, and its nature is stronger in analytical Virgo. Pure Mercurial expression becomes difficult in Sagittarius and in Pisces, which communicate and relate more through hopes and beliefs than through facts.

♀ **Venus**, the Roman goddess of beauty, is associated with the power of love, the power of attraction and cohesion and the power of quiet, gentle persuasion. It stimulates the desire to be sociable. Its influences include balancing, harmonizing, and peacemaking. It is symbolic of affection, sentiment, sympathy, romance, friendship, beauty, pleasure, music, manners, art, attractiveness, values, appreciation, and a sense of aesthetics.

If afflicted (adversely aspected to other planets), the affectionate, warm and sympathetic nature of Venus can be flirtatious, self-indulgent, sensual, vain, lazy, and irresponsible.

Venus rules placid Taurus as well as Libra, the sign of harmony. A strong Venus influence has a mellowing effect. The Venus nature is more than gentle—it is graceful and tactful. Venus is not easily expressed in the intense signs of Scorpio or Aries. Virgo, because of its excessive criticism and fussiness, can also inhibit the expression of Venus, whereas the loving nature of Pisces reinforces the Venusian influence.

♂ **Mars** is the complement of Venus. Mars is yang, positive, outgoing energy, masculine in nature. It is a planet of desire, energy, and action. As the ancient god of war, Mars represents struggles within and with others. It is closely related to our physical energy, and it rules our animal essence. Martian expressions include desire, courage, initiative, executive ability, assertiveness, aggressiveness, impulsiveness, adventurousness, self-will, resistance, rashness (leading to accidents), and aggressive sexual love.

Mars rules forceful Aries and determined Scorpio. The aggressive nature of Mars is also easily expressed in the ambitious sign of Capricorn. The driving force of Mars is restrained when it falls in the partnership sign, Libra, or the easygoing Taurus. The receptive nature of Cancer is also not compatible with the assertiveness of Mars.

♃ **Jupiter** is larger than all the other planets combined. It is symbolic of expansion, the higher mind, wisdom, enthusiasm, optimism, spontaneity, benevolence, generosity, the desire to gain through experience, and the urge to improve the state of things. Jupiter represents increase, opportunity, rewards, abundance, tolerance, charity, philanthropy, ethics, confidence, faith, idealism, aspiration, justice, loyalty, self-indulgence, extravagance, joviality, and conceit. Jupiter protects, assists, magnifies, inflates, gives, speculates, inspires, encourages, counsels, and philosophizes. It carries the ability to grow in physical, mental, and moral directions.

Jupiter is most at home in Sagittarius, where the desire for a variety of experiences can bring wisdom. Expansive Jupiter is limited by the trivial mental nature of Gemini. Virgo can impede Jupiter with its preoccupation with detail. Free-flowing, imaginative Pisces reinforces Jupiter.

♄ **Saturn** symbolizes the first law of manifestation—limitation. Saturn strengthens the personality through endurance and persistence. It focuses and concentrates energy. Saturn's contractive nature gives us the opportunity for introspection, meditation, and concentration—to work out karma in the process of evolution. The key to dealing with Saturn is discipline. Saturn requires caution, restraint, seriousness, and stability. It is also related to time, organization, consolidation, self-preservation, crystallization, ambition, responsibility, conventionality, pessimism, and perseverance. Saturn inhibits, delays, restricts, perfects, and deepens. It causes fear, worry, and anxiety.

Saturn is most compatible with Capricorn, the sign of material organization and practical ambition. Saturn is ill-expressed in Cancer where it becomes hypersensitive. Saturn exalts in the balancing act of Libra and finds the impulsive nature of Aries at odds with its cautious approach.

♅ **Uranus** has a nature similar to Mercury in its nervous and mental impact, but it is much more powerful, violent, fanatical, and harder to handle for the physical body. Uranus represents the freedom urge. It is the planet of extremes and sudden change. It's a force which destroys the old to allow room for the new. Uranus disrupts the constricting influence and crystallizations of Saturn. It displaces and overthrows the established attitudes which have outlived their usefulness. The old must be shattered before the new can come, but we are often fearful of new, unknown ways and reluctant to let go. Uranus makes us let go. It shakes us loose!

The nature of Uranus has an exciting, uprooting, and awakening effect. It brings disruption, anarchy, rebellion, revolution, freedom, individualism, altruism, originality, invention, experimentation, instability, erratic action, and detachment. It is related to intuitive knowledge.

♆ **Neptune** is often considered a higher vibration of Venus. It symbolizes receptivity, passivity, impressionability, and nebulousness. Neptune brings either spiritual strength or escapist tendencies—seeking the path of least resistance. Neptune can offer spiritual guidance and protection, or entice us to avoid all responsibility. Other Neptunian traits include being idealistic, imaginative, intuitive, subtle, artistically creative, evasive, deceitful (to yourself as well as to others), hypersensitive, sentimental, impractical, careless, scattered, indecisive, and compassionate. Neptune is the god of oceans. It rules the watery sign of Pisces and is inhibited in the earthy, orderly, practical, and constricting sign of Virgo, the opposite of Pisces. Neptune expresses its nature well through inspirational Sagittarius. It is constrained by the mundane level of the daily affairs of Gemini.

♀ **Pluto** can be considered the higher octave of Mars. Pluto represents those elements which have not yet been integrated into the collective consciousness—befitting its 2006 demotion to "minor planet" status. Pluto represents the urge to transform and to regenerate, bringing rebirth. It is a symbol of decay, contamination, infection, destruction, obsessions, desire, disintegration, and elimination, but also symbolizes a cleansing, healing catharsis.

Aspects

Planets form various angular relationships to each other, which are called aspects. Imagine an aspect as the blending rays of two planets.

✳ The **sextile**, 60°, is a favorable aspect, the planets usually being in congenial signs of compatible elements. This aspect can allow the influences of the planets to work in harmony. However, the sextile only brings opportunity. These opportunities must be acted upon to be of use.

☐ The **square**, 90°, is regarded as unfavorable. It represents the struggle of two forces at cross-purposes. The square brings stress and denotes obstacles which can inspire growth through concentrated effort.

△ The **trine**, 120°, the most harmonious aspect, usually joins planets in congenial signs of the same element. Energies combine with ease. The drawback is the lack of challenge—getting benefits without effort.

☍ The **opposition**, 180° (☍ = Lunar Eclipse), when planets are exactly opposite each other, causes stress and awareness. This polarity, though tense, does not have to be discordant as opposites are complementary.

☌ The **conjunction** (☌ = Solar Eclipse or Lunar occultation), is when two planets are at the same degree of longitude (or within orb). It gives great strength to the energies of the interacting planets and can be either harmonious or discordant depending upon the nature of the planets involved. More can be determined about the nature of a particular conjunction by comparing the nature of the sign in which it occurs to the natures of the planets involved. A planet strongly compatible to the sign of the conjunction can dominate the energies of the other planet.

Orbs: Aspects given in the calendar are listed at their exact times. This is when they are strongest, but the influences are present before and after the aspect is exact. This aura of influence is called the orb.

Delineation: Consider the meaning of the aspect, the natures and combined meanings of the planets, and the strength of the planets by virtue of their signs.

☽☌☿ **Moon conjunct Mercury:** Intellect and feelings are working together. Mentality is active, alert and sensitive. Nervous systems are highly tuned and very responsive. People are talkative and intellectually attuned to intuitions and emotions.

☽⚹☿, ☽△☿ Moon sextile or trine Mercury: Communication and conversation are easy with this positive connection of mind and emotions. Practical mental abilities and good common sense are highlighted. It is a good time to conduct business, utilize communications media, or use writing as a means of expression.

☽□☿, ☽☍☿ Moon square or opposite Mercury: Minds are acute but restless and excitable. Nervous systems function poorly. The unconscious mind will interfere with the conscious reasoning process. Preoccupation with the past can compromise one's objectivity and open-mindedness. Concern with trivialities and emotional whims might block meaningful mental pursuits. Incessant talking can drain everyone's energy. This is a very poor time for communications with the public. Nervous energy can cause digestive difficulties.

☽☌♀ Moon conjunct Venus: There is a good balanced outlook on life and a love of beauty. The emotional response to beauty and harmony heightens artistic abilities. Sensitivity and affections are strong as subconscious sensuality seeks emotional satisfaction. This is a good time for romance or for any social gathering. Have a party!

☽⚹♀, ☽△♀ Moon sextile or trine Venus: Generally similar to the conjunction, but more pronounced. Personalities mellow. Dispositions are pleasant. There is an increased interest in the arts.

☽□♀, ☽☍♀ Moon square or opposite Venus: There is an inability to express emotions and affections. There might be unhappiness and disappointments in emotional relationships. People become moody and overly sensitive. There are material and domestic difficulties. This is not recommended as a time for organizing social events.

☽☌♂ Moon conjunct Mars: Brings moodiness, aggressiveness, impulsive actions. Feelings are strong and outbursts of anger are likely. People seem opinionated and are also likely to feel courageous.

☽⚹♂, ☽△♂ Moon sextile or trine Mars: This brings good emotional and physical health, a lot of energy and emotional force. There are opportunities for material enterprises or for home improvements.

☽□♂, ☽☍♂ Moon square or opposite Mars: A time of delicate health and strong, volatile emotions. It is easy to be quarrelsome, get upset and lose tempers. People are irritable, impulsive and self-indulgent.

☽☌♃ Moon conjunct Jupiter: People are sympathetic and generous. There is concern for social welfare. This conjunction brings good health and optimism, and possibly an urge for change.

☽⚹♃, ☽△♃ Moon sextile or **trine Jupiter:** Brings pleasant temperaments and kind dispositions. Domestic peace and happiness become important. It is a good time for business.

☽□♃, ☽☍♃ Moon square or **opposite Jupiter:** Financial judgment is not good. Tendencies are towards extravagance, foolish generosity and laziness. Overeating is likely. Spiritual doubts may arise.

☽☌♄ Moon conjunct Saturn: Opportunity for hard work. Orderliness and duty become important. People are inclined to be critical and stingy, timid, cautious, and they may feel inadequate. Depression is very possible.

☽⚹♄, ☽△♄ Moon sextile or **trine Saturn:** Benefits come through a willing acceptance of duty. There can be gains by keeping things practical and orderly. Physical comforts seem of little importance.

☽□♄, ☽☍♄ Moon square or **opposite Saturn:** There is a lack of emotional flexibility or optimism. Depression looms. Judgmental attitudes may block abilities to respond to others in an appropriate way. Life is just hard.

☽☌♅ Moon conjunct Uranus: Be ready for sudden changes of mood and impulsive, unexpected actions. High emotional tension and freedom-seeking urges arise.

☽⚹♅, ☽△♅ Moon sextile or **trine Uranus:** Ambition and intuition are strong. Feelings of independence and self-reliance surface. There is much energy in the air. This aspect gives rise to an inventive, original, spontaneous imagination. Psychic abilities can become highly tuned. Changeable moods help break through inhibiting patterns, bringing opportunities to evolve. New friends are often found.

☽□♅, ☽☍♅ Moon square or **opposite Uranus:** Expect disruptions and obsessions with the unusual and unconventional. Independence is so important that communicative contact with others is difficult. People become restless, irritable, and stubborn and may be prone to accidents.

☽☌♆ Moon conjunct Neptune: A time of warmth, kindness, sympathy, and understanding. Emotions and psychic inclinations are strong and feelings are vulnerable. It is easy to drift into a dream world—Neptune makes people very impressionable. Check out the sign this aspect is in and how it relates to your natal chart.

☽⚹Ψ, ☽△Ψ **Moon sextile** or **trine Neptune:** Sensitivity opens the unconscious. Imagination is strong and inspirational.

☽☐Ψ, ☽☍Ψ **Moon square** or **opposite Neptune:** Self-deception is easy. Difficult emotional relationships and strong escapist tendencies arise.

☽☌♇ **Moon conjunct Pluto:** Moods and impulsiveness may lead to new emotional foundations.

☽⚹♇, ☽△♇ **Moon sextile** or **trine Pluto:** Strong emotional outbursts may be disruptive, but ultimately productive.

☽☐♇, ☽☍♇ **Moon square** or **opposite Pluto:** Emotions are stifled and people are uneasy. Jealousy is likely. Secrets may be revealed.

☽☌☉ **Moon conjunct Sun (New Moon):** Harmony, vitality, and determination increase as well as instinctual inclinations.

☽⚹☉, ☽△☉ **Moon sextile** or **trine Sun:** Feelings and thinking can be easily aligned. Inner conflicts are lifted. Ambition ebbs as the feeling of contentment rides high. Harmony is everywhere. People can "let it be."

☽☐☉ **Moon square Sun (First or Last Quarter):** Tensions and conflicts erupt between desires and emotions as people struggle for fulfillment.

☽☍☉ **Moon opposite Sun (Full Moon):** Emotions, self-confidence, and energy can go to extreme highs or lows as people crest on the waves of the preceding New Moon, and on the perspectives that have or haven't developed through the first two lunar phases.

Moon through the Signs

☽ in ♈ When the Moon passes through **Aries**, ruled by Mars, people are highly enthusiastic. It is a period of ambition and energetic activity. It is a good time for beginning projects and instigating change. Be aware that a desire for change will be based more upon impulse than reason. Watch for temperamental flare-ups and selfishness. With all this forceful energy, it is important to be mindful of the rights of others. Aries, which rules the head, is known for its headstrong behavior. While the Moon is in Aries people are susceptible to head injuries.

☽ in ♉ When the Moon goes into **Taurus**, the aggressive, charging Aries ram mellows into the solid, placid bull. Remember the term "bull-headed," as people will now tend to be very cautious and unchanging, leaning toward stubbornness. There is a feeling that it is necessary to protect the status quo or what one already has (key phrase is "I have"). The need for financial and material security is strong. While the Moon is in Taurus, take time to continue or finish projects already started. Venus rules Taurus, so this would be a good time to enjoy and appreciate the earthly beauty which surrounds us. Taurus rules the throat.

☽ in ♊ While the Moon is in the dualistic sign of **Gemini**, we may never make up our minds. With the Gemini ease of seeing both sides of everything, we feel more adaptable, changeable, and talkative. Gemini being ruled by Mercury makes this a time for communication. It is a good time to write, take care of puzzling tasks, make speeches, or just let ideas soar through the clouds. Intellectual pursuits and mind games may become more prominent than practical concerns. People begin to feel restless and there is an inclination to rationalize emotions. A spontaneous tongue may hastily express things that are only true for the moment. Gemini rules the lungs, arms, hands, and nervous system.

☽ in ♋ Since **Cancer** is ruled by the Moon, lunar influences are strongest and most easily expressed when focused through Cancer. The Moon greatly influences the personality, the subconscious and emotions, and it molds instinctual behavior. When the Moon is in Cancer, it is a time of intense emotions and great sensitivity with people responding to life through emotions rather than reason. During this very vulnerable period be cautious not to emotionally wound others nor to allow yourself to be wounded. Generally, people will be passive, easy-going, sentimental, loving, and nurturing. This motherly expression of caring is often expressed with food and it is easy to overeat. Cancer rules the breasts and stomach. Cancer is a nurturing sign and the most fertile sign of the zodiac.

☽ in ♌ Under the influence of the Moon in **Leo**, people need romance, affection, and recognition. The desire to be admired and appreciated can be so strong that it may result in especially dramatic behavior. Leo is ruled by the Sun, making this a time of ambition, independence, and leadership. People may refuse to recognize limitations. The Moon in Leo is a time of enjoyment and warmth, and a time to show kindness and generosity to others. Leo rules the heart and the upper spine.

☽ in ♍ **Virgo**, like Gemini, is ruled by Mercury. While the Moon is in Virgo, it is a good time for intellectual pursuits, more so for those requiring critical detail rather than innovative creativity. This is also a good time for taking care of any matter that requires painstaking attention. People may become shy and retiring with the Moon passing through Virgo, but also tend to be discriminating, fastidious, and overly critical. These influences lead to concern about food and health, as Virgo rules the intestines and the powers of assimilation. Many people feel the urge to clean up their homes at this time, which is a good way to channel Virgo energy.

☽ in ♎ While the Moon is in **Libra** people have a strong sensitivity to and attraction for others. This comes from the Libran search for harmony and balance, for the Libra nature accentuates teamwork. It brings opportunities to form partnerships of all kinds (friendships, marriage, business). Libra is ruled by Venus, which is manifested as a friendly and tolerant nature and a desire to beautify. It is an excellent time for artistic work as the beauty of Venus is combined with the intellectual ease of an air sign. This is a good time for a social gathering, when the consciousness of self, as expressed in the first six signs of the zodiac, becomes united with the awareness of the needs and desires of others. The Libra keynote is "I balance," as in yin/yang, day/night, me/you, summer/winter.

Libra rules the kidneys and lower back. Be careful not to imbibe too many impurities during this time when the kidneys are so vulnerable.

☽ in ♏ **Scorpio** is ruled by Mars and Pluto. Mars' influence brings out strong passions and Pluto shows very strong desires. People often get aggressive, critical, impatient, and moody. There is a marked increase of intensity and a heightened sensitivity to personal offenses and insults. Remember that Scorpio has a suspicious and secretive nature. Avoid social complications. Beware of jealousy. Watch out for the Scorpion sting. Remember to forgive and forget. Be cautious interacting with the opposite sex; however, it could be a good time for an intense merging with another on a deep emotional level. Scorpio rules the generative system, organs of reproduction, and the lower spine. The Moon in Scorpio is a very bad time for surgical operations.

☽ in ♐ The Moon in **Sagittarius** can give an idealistic feeling, or a sense of discontinuity, restlessness, desire for adventures and sports, a love of change and motion, and the itch to travel. People will be warm and friendly since Sagittarius is ruled by expansive Jupiter, but they may also have a strong need for independence and feel unable to endure restrictions.

People will likely feel spontaneous, intuitive (prophetic), and animated with a tendency toward superficial enthusiasm. Here the Moon stimulates our aspirations for self-improvement and brings a philosophical influence. It is a good time for intellectual affairs, promoting ideas through publishing, lecturing, etc., or dealing with institutions of learning. Sagittarius rules the thighs and hips.

☽ in ♑ With the Moon in **Capricorn** the vibrations of Saturn are emphasized. This brings contraction following Jupiter's expansive influence in Sagittarius. It's a time of material ambition, work, and duty. Spiritual and intellectual interests fall away. In the search for status and financial security, people may become insensitive, even unsympathetically cruel, but from perceived necessity rather than animosity.

The Saturn influence of Capricorn can cause pessimism or negative outlooks to creep in. While the Moon is in Capricorn energy is generally sluggish. It is a time to diligently apply ourselves to tasks while living solely in the present. Capricorn rules the knees, teeth, bones, and skin.

☽ in ♒ **Aquarius** is ruled by Uranus. While the Moon is in Aquarius, public affairs become more important as there is an increased interest in social welfare. People are very friendly, but in a superficial manner. Uranus brings the desire for freedom and a love for the innovative and unconventional. People are now operating from intellectual rather than emotional motivations. Searching for expression of personal thoughts and uniqueness, they may demand freedom to come and go without restrictions. Aquarius rules the ankles, the circulation, the electrical forces in the body, and the nervous system.

☽ in ♓ **Pisces** is ruled by Neptune, which brings an inclination toward psychic impressions. Imagination is strong and there is a heightened sensitivity to music and other intangible forces. There are tendencies to be emotional, spiritual, and self-sacrificing. A developing impressionability may cause feelings of vulnerability and withdrawal for emotional protection. People may feel passive, sentimental, gentle, kind, and cheerful, but too easily discouraged. Some people experience stirrings of vague memories (often identified as past lives) or insights into the spiritual meaning of current situations. Pisces rules the feet.

The Lunar Cycle

From New Moon to Full Moon, the first two quarters, the Moon is increasing in light, or waxing. This period of increasing light is traditionally the time for new beginnings, new projects, and ideas for growth. The waxing Moon is a time of spontaneous and instinctual action.

Should your new ideas or projects come to an impasse, this might be broken at the Full Moon. The waning Moon, from one Full Moon to the next New Moon, is a time for conscious growth as the Moon dissipates its collected solar potential. The time of the waxing Moon is in many traditions concerned more with mundane outer matters, whereas the period of the waning Moon deals with subconscious enlightenment leading to the clarification of conscious values. The waxing Moon brings instinctual growth. The waning Moon brings a conscious process of creative release.

The New Moon (☽☌☉) begins a new cycle. It is the seed of the beginning lunar cycle. The chart of the New Moon is the key to influences in the coming lunar month.

The First Quarter (☽□☉) is the beginning of the second phase. Beginning with the seed of the New Moon, growth in consciousness might be impeded by obstacles from the past. Ideally, these will be overcome by the First Quarter, a point of focus which illustrates the necessity for change. This must happen if the energy released with the coming Full Moon is to be utilized. If rejection of the shackles from the past is incomplete, then the illumination and growth offered during this cycle cannot be fully integrated. It may even sour. Whatever patterns are set at the First Quarter will continue to develop throughout the lunar cycle.

The Full Moon (☽☍☉) illuminates the seed and potential of the New Moon. The third quarter, Full Moon to Last Quarter, ideally brings clarification to the influences of the entire lunar cycle. If a positive attitude of growth has developed and if the restrictions of the past were thrown off during the waxing Moon, then the Full Moon can now bring fulfillment and a renewed sense of determination and resolve. However, if a negative attitude has dominated the period of increasing light, then the Full Moon might bring serious mental, and possibly physical, conflicts.

The fourth quarter is from the Last Quarter (☽□☉) to the next New Moon. It can bring a crisis in consciousness. This cycle's experiences have culminated and one must now prepare for rebirth as the process repeats itself with the next New Moon.

Moon Void of Course

As the Moon orbits the Earth it passes through the signs of the zodiac. Every lunar month it travels through all twelve signs, passing through each in more than two, but less than three days. When the Moon approaches the end of each sign, it goes beyond its last major aspect, or connection, with another planet. When this happens, and until it moves into the next sign, the Moon is said to be "Void of Course." This period is a time when we can feel uncomfortably disconnected and without direction. It is, therefore, an ideal time for centering ourselves.

The void of course condition may occur for only seconds or minutes of time or it may last for a day or two. It all depends on the locations of the planets and their interactions at the time.

While the Moon is void of course (V/c) it is wise to avoid making important decisions. Judgment at this time is probably faulty. Decisions tend to be unrealistic, subject to factors unknown at the time. New paths are likely to be plagued with false starts, errors, and unexpected hassles.

During Moon void of course, actions produce unforeseen, surprising results. Creative efforts go in unexpected directions. Contracts, promises or new laws bring on difficulties. Purchases prove to be unsatisfactory or the object simply does not fulfill its intention. Routines involving no decisions will usually go well but often require corrections later. Delays and frustrations are common. Moon void of course is a time to "kick back," let life flow and avoid putting yourself in the path of difficulties.

Presidential candidates Dewey, Nixon (vs. Kennedy), Goldwater, and McGovern were all nominated while the Moon was void of course. Every presidential candidate from the two major parties in 1900 until 1972 who was nominated while the Moon was void of course was defeated.

Nixon was reelected in 1972 while the Moon was void of course. And President Ford was sworn in while the Moon was void of course.

The important guideline for Moon void of course periods is to avoid being involved in concerns beyond your spiritual center. Moon void of course is a time for subjective, spiritual, non-materialistic concerns. If we have taken time off from business to give attention to relaxation and our spiritual growth during the Moon void of course, we can more effectively go back to dealing with the affairs of the day-to-day material world once the Moon has entered a new sign.

Planting by the Moon

The Moon governs growth. Planting is most productive if the lunar influences are considered. We have long heard sayings about planting by the light or dark of the Moon. These old sayings refer to the phases of the Moon, which are the angular relationships of the forces of the Sun and Moon. However, it is important to also consider the nature of the sign of the zodiac through which the Moon is passing.

For best results plant, graft or transplant annuals that bear above-ground crops during the Moon's first and second quarters. (An "annual" is a plant that completes the entire life cycle in one growing season.) During the first and second quarters, New Moon to Full Moon, the Moon is increasing in light. This is known as the waxing Moon.

Following the Full Moon are the third and the fourth quarters. This phase is the "dark of the Moon" or the waning Moon. The third quarter is the best time for pruning, the planting of biennials, perennials, bulbs, and root crops. These can also be planted in the fourth quarter if necessary. However, the fourth quarter is best suited for tilling and destroying weeds and pests. It is also the best phase for cultivation and harvesting. Remember, the New Moon to the Full Moon is the time to make new beginnings, the time to increase. The Full Moon to the next New Moon is a time to bring affairs together and to a close.

The bruised areas of fruit picked in the first and second quarters will rot more easily, whereas the bruised areas of fruit picked in the third and fourth quarters will dry. You can retard your lawn's growth by cutting the grass during the waning Moon. Conversely, you can stimulate its growth by cutting it during the waxing Moon. Timber will season better if it is cut in the fourth quarter in a barren sign.

The most fertile signs, the water signs Cancer, Scorpio, and Pisces, are best for planting. The signs Capricorn, Taurus, and Libra are the next best signs. Taurus and Capricorn will produce strong, hardy plants. For beautiful and fragrant flowers, plant while the Moon is in Libra, which is ruled by Venus, the goddess and planet of beauty. The least productive times for planting are Aries, Gemini, Leo, Virgo, Sagittarius, and Aquarius.

The first day the Moon is in a sign is better for planting than is the second. The second day is better than the third. The influence of each sign is greatly intensified when the Sun and Moon are in the same sign.

Time Corrections

Times given in this calendar are either **Pacific Standard Time** or **Pacific Daylight Saving Time.** Calculations given with each monthly calendar express Daylight Saving Time from the second Sunday in March through the first Sunday in November. If your locality is not using Daylight Saving Time, subtract one hour from the times given for that period.

Pacific Time is corrected to **Rocky Mountain Time** by adding one hour. For **Central Time**, add two hours. For **Eastern Time**, add three hours. For **Alaskan Time**, subtract one hour. For **Hawaii-Aleutian Time**, subtract two hours from Pacific Standard Time or three hours from Pacific Daylight Saving Time. For **Greenwich Mean Time**, add eight hours to Pacific Standard Time or seven hours to Pacific Daylight Saving Time.

For other localities, use the TIME ZONE MAP below. Count the number of zones your position is from Pacific Time (-8). Add (or subtract) one hour for each zone you are to the right (or left) of column "-8". The numbers at the top of the map are the longitudes of the Standard Meridians for each time zone.

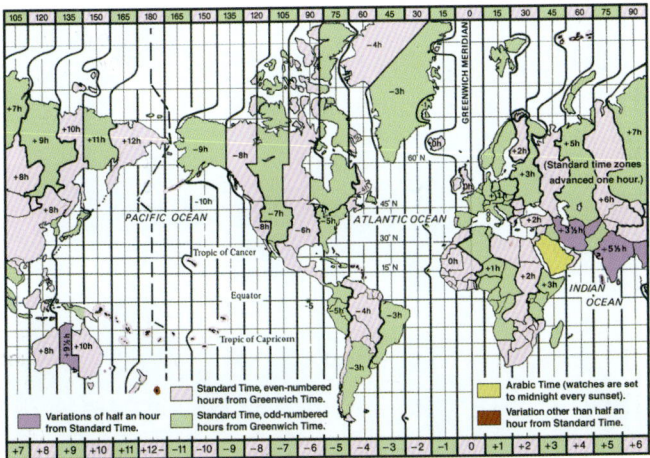

JANUARY 2012

Day	☉	☿	♀	♂	♃	♄	♅	♆	♇	Mean Node
1	11♑	21♐	15≈	20♍	00♉	28♎	01♈	29≈	07♑	13♐
2	12	23	16	20	00	28	01	29	07	13
3	13	24	17	21	01	28	01	29	07	13
4	14	25	19	21	01	29	01	29	07	13
5	16	27	20	21	01	29	01	29	08	13
6	17	28	21	21	01	29	01	29	08	12
7	18	00♑	22	22	01	29	01	29	08	12
8	18	01	24	22	01	29	01	29	08	12
9	19	03	25	22	01	29	01	29	08	12
10	20	04	26	22	01	29	01	29	08	12
11	21	05	27	23	02	29	01	29	08	12
12	22	07	08♓	23	02	29	02	29	08	12
13	23	08	00♓	23	02	29	02	29	08	12
14	24	09	01	23	02	29	02	29	08	12
15	25	11	02	23	02	29	02	29	08	12
16	26	13	03	23	02	29	02	30	08	12
17	27	15	05	23♍R	02	29	02	30	08	12
18	28	16	06	23	02	29	02	30	08	12
19	29	18	07	23	02	29	02	30	08	12
20	00≈	19	08	23	02	29	02	30	08	12
21	01	21	09	23	02	29	02	30	08	12
22	02	22	11	23	02	29	02	30	08	12
23	03	24	12	23	02	29	02	30	08	11
24	04	26	13	23♍R	02	29	02	30	08	11
25	05	27	14	23	02	29	02	30	08	11
26	06	29	16	23	03	29	02	30	08	11
27	07	00≈	17	23	03	29	02	30	08	11
28	08	02	18	23	03	29	02	30	08	11
29	09	04	19	23	03	29	02	30	08	11
30	10	05	20	22	03	29	02	30	08	11
31	11	07	21	22	03	29	02	30	08	11

Above are rounded to nearest whole degree. Positions more than 29°30' round to 30° of one sign before 00° of the next sign. See pages 50–61 for a complete ephemeris.

January Planting Days
Above-ground crops: Best: 8, 25, 26   Good days: 3, 4, 30, 31
Root crops/perennials: Best: 9, 16, 17, 18   Good: 14, 15, 21, 22
Planets Visible in the Morning Sky
Mercury through the 24th, Mars, and Saturn.
Planets Visible in the Evening Sky
Venus and Jupiter.

CAPRICORN ♑

December 21/22 to January 20   "I USE"

A cardinal, earth sign of negative polarity.

SYMBOL: the mountain goat with a dolphin's tail ascending the heights from the depths of the sea.

COLORS: dark shades.

RULING PLANET: Saturn.   RULES: the bones, skin, knees.

KEYWORDS: ambitious, conscientious, prudent, reliable, patient.

JANUARY 2012

1 ☽ in ♈ ☽✶♀ 7:03a ☽△☿ 8:56p New Year's Day	**2** ☽v/c 12:07p ☽→♉ 2:16p ☽☍♄ 11:01a ☽✶♆ 12:07p ☽☌♃ 3:14p	**3** ☽ in ♉ ☽△♇ 5:18a ☽△☉ 4:43p	**4** ☽ in ♉ ☽□♀ 2:49a ☽△♂ 8:38a	**5** ☽v/c 0:47a ☽→♊ 2:44a ☽□♆ 0:47a ☽✶♅ 4:36a	**6** ☽ in ♊ ☽△♀ 8:40p ☽□♂ 8:44p	**7** ☽v/c 11:52a ☽→♋ 1:05p ☿✶♄ 0:13a ☿✶♆ 7:16a ☽△♄ 10:35a ☽△♆ 11:21a ☽☍☿ 11:52a ☽✶♃ 2:20p ☽□♅ 2:58p ☿→♑ 10:34p
☽ in ♋ Full Moon 18♋26 11:30p ☽☍♇ 3:23a ☿△♃ 10:05a ☿□♅ 3:24p ☽☍☉ 11:30p	**9** ☽v/c 6:25p ☽→♌ 8:35p ☽✶♂ 5:48a ☽□♄ 6:25p ☽□♃ 9:59p ☽△♅ 10:29p	**10** ☽ in ♌ No exact aspects	**11** ☽ in ♌ ☽☍♀ 9:28p ☽✶♄ 11:49p	**12** ☽v/c 0:24a ☽→♍ 1:44a ☽☍♆ 0:24a ☽△♃ 3:18a ☽△☿ 1:33p ☽△♇ 3:11p ☉△♂ 8:46p	**13** ☽ in ♍ ☽v/c 5:58p ♀△♄ 1:05a ☿☌♇ 5:01a ♀☌♆ 7:18a ☽☌♂ 4:36p ☽△☉ 5:58p ♀→♓ 9:47p	**14** ☽→♎ 5:28a ☽☍♅ 7:28a ♀✶♃ 6:49p ☽□♇ 6:49p ☽□☿ 11:15p
15 ☽ in ♎ No exact aspects	Last Qtr 25♎38 1:08a ☽v/c 7:29a ☽→♏ 8:33a ☽□☉ 1:08a ☽☌♄ 7:00a ☽△♆ 7:29a ☽☍♃ 10:34a ☽△♀ 2:05p ☽✶♇ 9:57p Martin L. King Jr. Day	**17** ☽ in ♏ ☽✶☿ 8:24a ☽✶♂ 11:24p	**18** ☽v/c 10:32a ☽→♐ 11:29a ☽✶☉ 8:00a ☽□♆ 10:32a ☽△♅ 1:41p ☽□♀ 9:47p	**19** ☽ in ♐ ☉□♄ 1:20p	**20** ☽v/c 1:50p ☽→♑ 2:40p ☽□♂ 2:42a ☉→♒ 8:10a ♀✶♇ 12:31p ☽✶♄ 1:21p ☽✶♆ 1:50p ☽□♅ 5:02p ☽△♃ 5:17p **Sun enters Aquarius**	**21** ☽ in ♑ ☽☌♇ 4:31a ☽✶♀ 6:00a ☉✶♅ 5:21p ☉□♃ 10:35p
New Moon 2♒42 11:39p ☽v/c 5:38p ☽→♒ 6:53p ☽☌☿ 4:02a ☽△♂ 6:42a ☽□♄ 5:38p ☽✶♅ 9:27p ☽□♃ 9:56p ☽☌☉ 11:39p	**23** ☽ in ♒ ☿△♂ 3:17a ♂SR 4:54p Chinese New Year: the Dragon	**24** ☽ in ♒ ☽△♄ 11:59p	**25** ☽v/c 0:34a ☽→♓ 1:11a ☽☌♆ 0:34a ☽✶♃ 4:47a ☽✶♇ 4:30p	**26** ☽ in ♓ ☽v/c 8:52p ☽☌♀ 5:12a ☽☍♂ 8:52p	**27** ☽→♈ 10:28a ☿□♄ 1:21a ☿→♒ 10:12a ☽✶☿ 10:30a ☽☌♅ 1:39p	**28** ☽ in ♈ ☽✶☉ 2:01a ☽□♇ 2:47a ☿✶♅ 10:27a ☿□♃ 8:08p
29 ☽v/c 10:09p ☽→♉ 10:28p ☽☍♄ 9:21p ☽✶♆ 10:09p	☽ in ♉ First Qtr 10♉41 8:10p ☽☌♃ 3:29a ☽□☿ 8:14a ☽△♇ 3:25p ☽□☉ 8:10p	**31** ☽ in ♉ ☽✶♀ 6:08p ☽△♂ 8:28p				

CAPRICORN

AQUARIUS

DECEMBER 2011

S	M	T	W	T	F	S
				1	2	3
4	5	6	7	8	9	10
11	12	13	14	15	16	17
18	19	20	21	22	23	24
25	26	27	28	29	30	31

FEBRUARY 2012

S	M	T	W	T	F	S
			1	2	3	4
5	6	7	8	9	10	11
12	13	14	15	16	17	18
19	20	21	22	23	24	25
26	27	28	29			

Moon goes void-of-course.
Moon enters next sign.

New Moon 2♒42 11:39p
☽v/c 5:38p
☽→♒ 6:53p
☽☌☿ 4:02a
☽△♂ 6:42a
☽□♄ 5:38p
☽✶♅ 9:27p
☽□♃ 9:56p
☽☌☉ 11:39p

Daily aspects (when exact)
Sign or Direction changes

Pacific Standard Time

Day	☉	☿	♀	♂	♃	♄	♅	♆	♇	Mean Node
1	13♒	09♒	23♈	23R♍	03♉	29♎	02♈	30♒	08♑	11♐
2	14	10	25	22	03	29	02	30	08	11
3	15	12	26	22	03	29	02	00♓	08	11
4	16	14	27	22	03	29	02	00	08	11
5	17	16	29	22	04	29	02	00	09	11
6	18	17	00♉	21	04	29	02	00	09	11
7	19	19	02	21	04	29	02	01	09	11
8	20	21	03	21	04	29R	02	01	09	11
9	21	23	04	21	04	29	02	01	09	11
10	22	24	06	20	05	29	02	01	09	11
11	23	26	07	20	05	29	02	01	09	11
12	24	28	08	20	05	29	03	01	09	10
13	25	00♓	09	19	05	29	03	01	09	10
14	26	04	11	19	05	29	03	01	09	10
15	27	05	12	19	06	29	03	01	09	10
16	28	07	13	18	06	29	03	01	09	10
17	28	09	15	17	06	29	03	01	09	10
18	00♓	11	16	17	06	29	03	01	09	10
19	01	11	14	16	06	29	03	01	09	10
20	02	13	15	16	07	29	03	01	09	10
21	03	15	17	16	07	29	03	01	09	10
22	04	16	18	17	07	29	03	01	09	10
23	05	18	19	17	07	29	03	01	09	10
24	06	20	21	16	07	29	03	01	09	10
25	07	21	22	16	07	29	03	01	09	10
26	08	23	23	16	06	29	03	01	09	10
27	09	25	25	15	07	29	03	01	09	10
28	10	26	26	15	07	29	03	01	08	10
29	11	28	28	15	07	29	03	01	08	10

Above are rounded to nearest whole degree. Positions more than 29°30′ round to 30° of one sign before 00° of the next sign. See pages 50–61 for a complete ephemeris.

February Planting Days
Above-ground crops: Best: 4, 5, 22, 23   Good days: 26, 27, 28
Root crops & perennials: Best: 13, 14, 21   Good: 11, 12, 17, 18

Planets Visible in the Morning Sky
   Mars and Saturn.

Planets Visible in the Evening Sky
   Mercury from the 19th, Venus, and Jupiter.

AQUARIUS ♒
January 20 to February 18/19 "I KNOW"
A fixed, air sign of positive polarity.
SYMBOL: the water bearer—the energy bearer.
COLORS: iridescent blues.   RULING PLANETS: Saturn and Uranus.
RULES: the circulation and the ankles.

FEBRUARY 2012

			1 ☽v/c 11:06a ☽→♊ 11:15a AQUARIUS ☽□♆ 11:06a ☽✱♅ 2:54p ♀☍♂ 3:41p	**2** ☽ in ♊ ☽△☿ 6:41a Candlemas ☽△☉ 2:01p Groundhog Day	**3** ☽v/c 9:06p ☽→♋ 10:04p ☽□♂ 7:24a ♆→♓ 10:52a ☽□♀ 12:03p ☽△♄ 9:06p ☽△♆ 10:06p	**4** ☽ in ♋ ☽□♅ 1:43a ☽✱♃ 3:53a ☽☍♇ 2:06p
5 ☽ in ♋ ☽✱♂ 3:01p	**6** ☽v/c 4:31a ☽→♌ 5:24a ☽△♀ 1:28a ☽□♄ 4:31a ☽△♅ 9:00a ☽□♃ 11:23a	☽ in ♌ Full Moon 18♌32 1:54p ☉☌☿ 1:03a ♄SR 6:03a ☽☍☉ 1:54p ☽☍☿ 2:41p ♀→♈ 10:01p	**8** ☽v/c 8:42a ☽→♍ 9:32a ☽✱♄ 8:42a ☽☍♆ 9:52a ☽△♃ 3:45p	**9** ☽ in ♍ ☽v/c 9:11p ☽△♇ 0:08a ♀☌♅ 6:30p ☽☌♂ 9:11p	**10** ☽→♎ 11:54a ☽☍♅ 3:36p ☽☍♀ 5:24p	**11** ☽ in ♎ ☽□♇ 2:23a
12 ☽v/c 1:09p ☽→♏ 2:01p ☽△☉ 2:27a ☽△☿ 9:59a ☽☌♄ 1:09p ☽△♆ 2:36p ☽☍♃ 9:12p	**13** ☽ in ♏ ☽✱♇ 4:45a ☿△♄ 10:44a ☿→♓ 5:38p ☿☌♆ 10:48p	☽v/c 9:04a ☽→♐ 4:56p Last Qtr 25♏24 9:04a ☽✱♂ 0:07a ☽□☉ 9:04a ☽□♆ 5:40p ☽□☿ 8:28p ☽△♅ 9:06p St. Valentine's Day	**15** ☽ in ♐ ☽△♀ 7:53a ♀□♇ 10:31a	**16** ☽v/c 8:03p ☽→♑ 9:03p ☽□♂ 2:47a ☿✱♃ 8:07a ☽✱☉ 5:08p ☽✱♄ 8:03p ☽✱♆ 9:57p	**17** ☽ in ♑ ☽□♅ 1:30a ☽△♃ 5:44a ☽✱☿ 8:51a ☽☌♇ 12:41p ☽□♀ 5:17p	**18** ☽ in ♑ ☽△♂ 6:33a ☉△♄ 8:02a ☿✱♇ 1:23p ☉→♓ 10:18p **Sun enters Pisces**
19 ☽v/c 1:22a ☽→♒ 2:28a ☽□♄ 1:22a ☽✱♅ 7:14a ☽□♃ 12:02p ☉☌♆ 12:42p	**20** ☽ in ♒ ☽✱♀ 4:28a Presidents Day	☽v/c 8:17a ☽→♓ 9:31a New Moon 2♓42 2:35p ☽△♄ 8:17a ☽☌♆ 10:48a ☽☌☉ 2:35p Mardi Gras ☽✱♃ 8:09p Shrove Tuesday	**22** ☽ in ♓ ☽v/c 6:24p ☽✱♇ 2:23a ☽☌☿ 4:35p ☽☍♂ 6:24p Ash Wednesday	**23** ☽→♈ 6:48p PISCES ☿☍♂ 3:25a	**24** ☽ in ♈ ☽☌♅ 0:26a ☽□♇ 12:31p	**25** ☽ in ♈ ☉✱♃ 2:34a ☽☌♀ 11:00a
26 ☽v/c 4:52a ☽→♉ 6:29a ☽☍♄ 4:52a ☽✱♆ 8:15a ☽☌♃ 7:43p ☽✱☉ 10:53p	**27** ☽ in ♉ ☽△♇ 0:54a ☽△♂ 2:08p ☉✱♇ 11:14p	**28** ☽v/c 11:46a ☽→♊ 7:27p ☽✱☿ 11:46a ☽□♆ 9:24p	☽ in ♊ First Qtr 10♊52 5:21p ☽✱♅ 1:49a ☽□☉ 5:21p		JANUARY 2012 / MARCH 2012 (see below)	Legend (see below)

JANUARY 2012

S	M	T	W	T	F	S
1	2	3	4	5	6	7
8	9	10	11	12	13	14
15	16	17	18	19	20	21
22	23	24	25	26	27	28
29	30	31				

MARCH 2012

S	M	T	W	T	F	S
				1	2	3
4	5	6	7	8	9	10
11	12	13	14	15	16	17
18	19	20	21	22	23	24
25	26	27	28	29	30	31

Moon goes void-of-course.
Moon enters next sign.
☽v/c 9:04a
☽→♐ 4:56p
Last Qtr
25♏24
9:04a
☽✱♂ 0:07a
☽□☉ 9:04a
☽□♆ 5:40p
☽□☿ 8:28p
☽△♅ 9:06p
St. Valentine's Day
Daily aspects (when exact)
Sign or Direction changes

MARCH 2012

Day	☉	☿	♀	♂	♃	♄	♅	♆	♇	Mean Node
1	12♓	29♓	26♈	14R	07♉	29R	03♈	01♓	09♑	10♐
2	13	01♈	27	14♍	07	29♎	03	01	09	10
3	14	02	28	14	08	29	03	01	09	10
4	15	03	30	13	08	29	03	01	09	10
5	16	04	01♉	13	08	29	03	01	09	10
6	17	05	02	12	08	29	03	01	09	09
7	18	05	03	12	08	29	04	01	09	09
8	19	06	04	12	09	29	04	01	09	09
9	20	06	05	11	09	29	04	01	09	09
10	21	07	06	11	09	29	04	01	09	09
11	22	07	07	10	09	29	04	01	09	09
12	23	07R	08	10	09	29	04	01	09	09
13	24	07	09	10	09	28	04	01	09	09
14	25	06	10	09	10	28	04	01	09	09
15	26	06	11	09	10	28	04	02	09	09
16	27	05	12	09	10	28	04	02	09	09
17	28	05	14	08	10	28	04	02	09	09
18	29	04	15	08	11	28	04	02	09	09
19	00♈	03	16	08	11	28	04	02	09	09
20	01	02	17	07	11	28	04	02	09	09
21	02	01	18	07	11	28	04	02	09	09
22	03	00	19	07	11	28	04	02	09	09
23	04	30♓	20	07	12	28	04	02	09	09
24	05	29	21	06	12	28	05	02	09	09
25	06	28	22	06	12	28	05	02	09	08
26	07	27	23	06	12	28	05	02	09	08
27	08	26	24	06	12	28	05	02	09	08
28	09	26	25	05	13	27	05	02	10	08
29	10	25	26	05	13	27	05	02	10	08
30	11	25	27	05	13	27	05	02	10	08
31	12	24	28	05	13	27	05	02	10	08

Above are rounded to nearest whole degree. Positions more than 29°30' round to 30° of one sign before 00° of the next sign. See pages 50–61 for a complete ephemeris.

March Planting Days

Above-ground crops: Best: 2, 3, 4, 30, 31 Good days: 25, 26
Root crops/perennials: Best: 11, 12, 20, 21 Good: 9, 10, 15, 16

Planets Visible in the Morning Sky

Mercury after the 29th, Mars through the 3rd, and Saturn.

Planets Visible in the Evening Sky

Mercury through the 14th, Venus, Mars from the 3rd, and Jupiter. **Do not confuse** Venus with Jupiter mid-month; Venus is brighter.

PISCES ♓

February 18/19 to March 19/20 "I BELIEVE"

A mutable, water sign of negative polarity.

SYMBOL: two fish swimming in opposite directions, and not seeing each other.

COLORS: sea greens.

RULING PLANET: Neptune. RULES: the feet.

MARCH 2012

MARCH 2012	Moon goes void-of-course Moon enters next sign. ☽v/c 1:39a ☽→♎ 8:50p Full Moon 18♍13 1:39a Purim ☽☍☉ 1:39a Int'l Women's Day Daily aspects (when exact) Sign or Direction changes	**FEBRUARY 2012** S M T W T F S 1 2 3 4 5 6 7 8 9 10 11 12 13 14 15 16 17 18 19 20 21 22 23 24 25 26 27 28 29 **APRIL 2012** S M T W T F S 1 2 3 4 5 6 7 8 9 10 11 12 13 14 15 16 17 18 19 20 21 22 23 24 25 26 27 28 29 30	**1** ☽ in ♊ ☽□♂ 0:53a	**2** ☽v/c 5:14a ☽→♋ 7:08a ☽✱♀ 0:29a ☿→♈ 3:41a ☽△♄ 5:14a ☽□☿ 7:33a ☽△♆ 9:11a ☽□♅ 1:29p ☽✱♃ 9:27p	**3** ☽ in ♋ ☽☍♇ 0:46a ☽△☉ 8:58a ☽✱♂ 9:18a ☉☍♂ 12:10p
4 ☽v/c 2:17p ☽→♌ 3:18p ♀☍♄ 3:18a ☽□♄ 1:20p ☽□♀ 2:17p ☽△☿ 8:57p ☽△♅ 9:25p	**5** ☽ in ♌ ♀→♉ 2:25a ☿☌♅ 3:36a ☽□♃ 5:20a	**6** ☽v/c 5:27p ☽→♍ 7:27p ♀✱♆ 4:27a ☽✱♄ 5:27p ☽☍♆ 9:30p ☽△♀ 10:52p	**7** ☽ in ♍ ☽△♃ 9:17a ☽△♇ 10:54a ☽☌♂ 3:28p	**8** Full Moon 18♍13 1:39a ☽v/c 1:39a ☽→♎ 8:50p Purim ☽☍☉ 1:39a Int'l Women's Day	**9** ☽ in ♎ PISCES ☽☍♅ 2:44a ☽☍☿ 7:01a ☽□♇ 11:53a	**10** ☽v/c 7:09p ☽→♏ 9:24p ☽☌♄ 7:09p ☽△♆ 11:38p
11 ☽ in ♏ ☽☍♀ 9:31a ☽☍♃ 1:13p ☽✱♇ 1:37p ☽✱♂ 3:33p Daylight Saving begins	**12** ☽v/c 11:30a ☽→♐ 11:53p ☿SR 0:49a ☽△☉ 11:30a ♃△♇ 9:31p	**13** ☽ in ♐ ☽□♆ 2:20a ☽△♅ 6:25a ☽△☿ 11:09a ☽□♂ 4:23p ♀△♇ 6:26p ♀☌♃ 10:54p	**14** Last Qtr 24♐52 6:25p ☽ in ♐ ♀△♂ 0:29a ♂△♃ 2:51a ♂△♇ 5:32p ☽□☉ 6:25p	**15** ☽v/c 0:34a ☽→♑ 3:24a ☽✱♄ 0:34a ☽✱♆ 6:05a ☽□♅ 10:26a ☽□☿ 1:53p ☽△♂ 7:18p ☽☌♇ 8:00p ☽△♃ 8:59p	**16** ☽ in ♑ ☽△♀ 0:11a	**17** ☽v/c 6:00a ☽→♒ 9:11a ☽✱☉ 4:12a ☽□♄ 6:00a ☽✱♅ 4:45p ☽✱☿ 5:46p St. Patrick's Day
18 ☽ in ♒ ☽□♃ 4:23a ☿☌♅ 10:24a ☽□♀ 11:39a	**19** ☽v/c 1:31p ☽→♓ 5:05p ☽△♄ 1:31p ☽☌♆ 8:17p ☉→♈ 10:15p **Vernal Equinox** **Sun enters Aries**	**20** ☽ in ♓ ☽☍♂ 7:25a ☽✱♇ 11:06a ☽✱♃ 1:55p	**21** ☽ in ♓ ☽v/c 1:39a ☽✱♀ 1:39a ☉☌☿ 12:22p	**22** New Moon 2♈22 7:37a ☽→♈ 2:57a ☽☌☿ 4:50a ☽☌☉ 7:37a ☽☌♅ 11:36a ☽□♇ 9:38p	**23** ☽ in ♈ ARIES ☿→♓ 6:22a	**24** ☽v/c 10:17a ☽→♉ 2:43p ☽☍♄ 10:17a ☉☌♅ 11:21a ☽✱♆ 6:28p
25 ☽ in ♉ ☽△♂ 3:13a ☽△♇ 9:57a ☽☌♃ 3:02p	**26** ☽ in ♉ ☽v/c 9:35p ☽☌♀ 12:26p ☽✱☿ 9:35p	**27** ☽→♊ 3:43a ☽□♆ 7:40a ☽✱♅ 1:15p ☽□♂ 3:04p ☽✱☉ 7:38p	**28** ☽ in ♊ No exact aspects	**29** ☽v/c 11:05a ☽→♋ 4:07p ☽□☿ 7:05a ☿✱♀ 10:43a ☽△♄ 11:05a ☉□♇ 12:54p ☽△♆ 8:06p	**30** First Qtr 10♋30 12:41p ☽ in ♋ ☽□♅ 1:38a ☽✱♂ 2:06a ☽☍♇ 10:47a ☽□☉ 12:41p ☽✱♃ 5:41p	**31** ☽ in ♋ ☽v/c 9:20p ☽△☿ 3:13p ☽□♄ 8:33p ☽✱♀ 9:20p

Pacific Daylight Saving Time begins 2:00AM March 11th. Set clocks ahead one hour.

Day	☉	☿	♀	♂	♃	♄	♅	♆	♇	Mean Node
1	13♈	24♓R	28♉	05♍R	14♉	27♎R	05♈	02♓	10♑	08♐
2	14	24R	29	05	14	27	05	02	10	08
3	15	24R	00Ⅱ	05	14	27	05	02	10	08
4	16	24♓D	01	04	15	27	05	02	10	08
5	17	24	02	04	15	27	05	02	10	08
6	18	24	03	04	15	27	05	02	10	08
7	19	25	04	04	15	26	05	02	10	08
8	20	25	05	04	16	26	05	02	10	08
9	21	26	06	04	16	26	06	02	10	08
10	22	27	08	04	16	26	06	02	10R	08
11	23	28	09	04	16	26	06	03	10	08
12	24	29	10	04	17	26	06	03	10	07
13	24	00♈	11	04D	17	26	06	03	10	07
14	25	02	12	04	17	26	06	03	09	07
15	26	03	13	04	17	25	06	03	09	07
16	27	05	14	04	18	25	06	03	09	07
17	28	07	15	04	18	25	06	03	09	07
18	29	09	16	04	18	25	06	03	09	07
19	00♉	11	17	04	18	25	06	03	09	07
20	00	13	18	04	18	25	06	03	09	07
21	01	15	19	04	19	25	07	03	09	07
22	02	17	19	04	19	25	07	03	09	07
23	03	19	20	04	19	25	07	03	09	07
24	04	22	21	05	19	25	07	03	09	07
25	05	24	22	05	20	24	07	03	09	07
26	06	26	22	05	20	24	07	03	09	07
27	07	29	23	05	20	24	07	03	09	07
28	08	01♉	23	05	20	24	07	03	09	07
29	09	03	24	05	20	24	07	03	09	07
30	10	06	25	05	20	24	07	03	09	07

Above are rounded to nearest whole degree. Positions more than 29°30' round to 30° of one sign before 00° of the next sign. See pages 50–61 for a complete ephemeris.

April Planting Days

Above-ground crops: Best: 26, 27   Good days: 5, 6, 21, 22
Root crops/perennials: Best: 7, 8, 16, 17   Good days: 11, 12, 13

Planets Visible in the Morning Sky
   Mercury, and Saturn through the 15th.
Planets Visible in the Evening Sky
   Venus, Mars, Jupiter through the 29th, and Saturn from the 15th.

ARIES ♈

March 19/20 to April 19 "I AM"

A cardinal, fire sign of positive polarity.
SYMBOL: the ram, lowering its head and blindly charging through.
COLORS: reds.   RULING PLANET: Mars.   RULES: the head.

APRIL 2012

1 ☽→♌ 1:35a ☽△♅10:42a Palm Sunday All Fools' Day	**2** ☽ in ♌ ARIES ☽△☉ 1:11a ☽□♃ 2:19a	**3** ☽v/c 6:47a ☽→♍ 6:53a ☽⚹♄ 1:57a ☽□♀ 6:47a ♀→♊ 8:18a ☽☍♆10:34a ☽☌♂ 2:16p ☽△♇ 11:01p	**4** ☽ in ♍ ☽v/c 10:37p ☿SD 3:11a ☽△♃ 6:35a ☽☍☿ 10:37p	**5** ☽→♎ 8:32a ☽△♀ 11:41a ☽☍♅ 4:54p ♀□♆ 6:51p ☽□♇ 11:51p	☽ in ♎ Full Moon 17♎23 12:19p ☽☍☉12:19p Good Friday	**7** ☽v/c 3:15a ☽→♏ 8:18a ☽☌♄ 3:15a ☽△♆ 11:54a ☽⚹♂ 2:31p ♀□♂ 4:37p ☽⚹♇ 11:27p Passover
8 ☽ in ♏ ☽v/c 11:56p ☽☍♃ 8:08a ☽△☿ 11:56p Easter Sunday	**9** ☽→♐ 8:12a ♀⚹♅ 9:52a ☽□♆12:00p ☽□♂ 2:22p ☽△♅ 5:02p ☽☍♀ 5:27p	**10** ☽ in ♐ ♇SR 9:21a ☽△☉ 7:51p	**11** ☽v/c 4:05a ☽→♑10:02a ☽□☿ 3:06a ☽⚹♄ 4:05a ☽⚹♆ 2:07p ☽△♂ 4:23p ☽□♅ 7:33p	**12** ☽ in ♑ ☽●♇ 2:30a ☽△♃ 1:44p	☽v/c 10:05a ☽→♒ 2:48p Last Qtr 23♑55 3:50a ☽□☉ 3:50a ☽□♄ 8:12a ☽⚹☿10:05a ♂SD 8:53p	**14** ☽ in ♒ ☽⚹♅ 1:07a ☽△♀ 8:10a ☽□♃ 9:10p Pan American Day
15 ☽v/c 3:42p ☽→♓10:38p ☉☍♄11:27a ☽△♄ 3:20p ☽⚹☉ 3:42p	**16** ☽ in ♓ ☽☌♆ 3:26a ☽☍♂ 5:44a ☿→♈ 3:42p ☽⚹♇ 4:58p ☽□♀ 8:40p Emancipation Day	**17** ☽ in ♓ ☽v/c 7:34a Tax Day ☽⚹♃ 7:34a	**18** ☽→♈ 8:59a ☽☌☿12:28p ☽☌♅ 8:45p	**19** ☽ in ♈ ☽□♇ 3:56a ☉→♉ 9:12a ☽⚹♀11:40a **Sun enters Taurus**	**20** ☽v/c 12:35p ☽→♉ 9:05p ☽☍♄12:35p	☽ in ♉ New Moon 1♉35 0:18a ☽☌☉ 0:18a ☽⚹♆ 2:25a ☽△♂ 5:12a ☽△♇ 4:25p April Lyrids Meteors
22 ☽ in ♉ ☽v/c 10:10a ☉⚹♆ 2:20a ☽☌♃10:10a ☿☌♅ 1:30p Earth Day	**23** ☽→♊10:05a ☽□♆ 3:33p ☉△♂ 5:59p ☽□♂ 6:46p ☽⚹♅10:42p	**24** ☽ in ♊ TAURUS ☽⚹☿ 2:17a ☽☌♀ 8:36p	**25** ☽v/c 1:31p ☽→♋10:42p ☿□♇ 7:50a ☽△♄ 1:31p Secretary's Day	**26** ☽ in ♋ ☽△♆ 4:10a ☽⚹♂ 7:50a ☽□♅ 11:17a ☽⚹☉12:31p ☽☍♇ 5:31p ☽□☿ 9:34p	**27** ☽ in ♋ ☽⚹♃12:59p	**28** ☽v/c 0:05a ☽→♌ 9:10a ☽□♄ 0:05a ☽△♅ 9:18p
☽ in ♌ First Qtr 9♌29 2:57a ☉△♇ 2:33a ☽□☉ 2:57a ☽△☿ 1:31p ☽⚹♀ 9:55p ☽□♃10:14p	**30** ☽v/c 7:17a ☽→♍ 4:02p ☽⚹♄ 7:17a ☽☍♆ 9:01p				**MARCH 2012** S M T W T F S 1 2 3 4 5 6 7 8 9 10 11 12 13 14 15 16 17 18 19 20 21 22 23 24 25 26 27 28 29 30 31 **MAY 2012** S M T W T F S 1 2 3 4 5 6 7 8 9 10 11 12 13 14 15 16 17 18 19 20 21 22 23 24 25 26 27 28 29 30 31	Moon goes void-of-course, Moon enters next sign. ☽v/c 10:05a ☽→♒ 2:48p Last Qtr 23♑55 3:50a ☽□☉ 3:50a ☽□♄ 8:12a ☽⚹☿ 10:05a ♂SD 8:53p Daily aspects (when exact) Sign or Direction changes

Pacific Daylight Saving Time

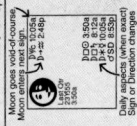

Above are rounded to nearest whole degree. Positions more than 29°30' round to 30° of one sign before 00° of the next sign. See pages 50-61 for a complete ephemeris.

Day	☉	☿	♀	♂	♃	♄	♅	♆	♇	Mean Node
1	12♉	18♈	21♊	05♍	20♉	25♏R	07♈	03♓	09♑R	07♐
2	13	20	22	06	21	25	07	03	09	06
3	14	21	22	06	21	25	07	03	09	06
4	15	23	23	06	21	25	07	03	09	06
5	16	25	23	07	22	25	07	03	09	06
6	17	26	23	07	22	25	07	03	09	06
7	18	28	23	07	22	24	07	03	09	06
8	19	00♉	24	08	22	24	07	03	09	06
9	20	01	24	08	23	24	07	03	09	06
10	21	03	24	08	23	24	07	03	09	06
11	22	05	24	09	23	24	07	03	09	06
12	23	07	24	09	23	24	07	03	09	06
13	24	09	24	10	23	24	07	03	09	06
14	25	11	24R	11	24	24	07	03	09	06
15	26	12	24	11	24	24	07	03	09	06
16	27	14	24	11	24	24	07	03	09	06
17	28	16	23	12	25	24	07	03	09	06
18	29	18	23	12	25	24	07	03	09	06
19	29	21	22	13	25	24	07	03	09	06
20	00♊	23	21	13	25	23	07	03	09	05
21	01	25	21	14	26	23	08	03	09	05
22	02	27	20	14	26	23	08	03	09	05
23	03	29	20	14	26	23	08	03	09	05
24	04	01♊	19	15	27	23	08	03	09	05
25	05	03	19	15	27	23	08	03	09	05
26	06	06	19	15	27	23	08	03	09	05
27	07	07	18	13	27	23	08	03	09	05
28	08	08	18	14	27	23	08	03	09	05
29	09	10	18	14	28	23	08	03	09	05
30	10	13	18	15	28	23	08	03	09	05
31	11	16	19	15	28	23	08	03	09	05

May Planting Days

Above-ground crops: Best: 5, 23, 24, 25　　Good: 3, 4, 30, 31
Root crops/perennials: Best: 6, 13, 14, 15　　Good: 9, 10, 18, 19, 20

Planets Visible in the Morning Sky
　Mercury through the 20th and Jupiter from the 28th.
Planets Visible in the Evening Sky
　Venus through the 30th, Mars, and Saturn.

TAURUS ♉

April 19 to May 20 "I HAVE"

A fixed, earth sign of negative polarity.
SYMBOL: the bull.　COLORS: pink and blue.　RULING PLANET: Venus.
RULES: the throat, cerebellum, and back part of the brain.

MAY 2012

SUNDAY	MONDAY	TUESDAY	WEDNESDAY	THURSDAY	FRIDAY	SATURDAY
		1 — May Day · D in ♍ — D♂♀ 1:27a · D△♀ 8:30a · D□♄ 12:34p	**2** — D▽♇ 3:58a · D→♉ 7:04p	**3** — D△♂ 3:21a · D□♀ 3:58a	**4** — D in ♉ — D✶☿ 5:10a · D⚹♆ 10:10a · D□♅ 6:09p · D♂♄ 8:35p	**5** — Full Moon 16♏21 8:35p · Cinco de Mayo — D▽♇ 5:52p
6 — D▽♃ 5:14a · D→♐ 6:39p	**7** — D in ♐	**8** — D△♃ 7:39a · D✶♅ 9:58a · D△♀ 6:34p · D♂♆ 10:15p · D□♄ 11:54p	**9** — D in ♑ — D♂♄ 6:32a · D△♆ 6:59a · D□☿ 10:33a	**10** — D⚹♆ 5:58a · D→≈ 10:03p — D in ♑	**11** — D in ≈ — D▽♃ 5:52p	**12** — Last Qtr 22♒33 2:47p · D in ≈
13 — Mother's Day — D△♃ 6:24a · D□♅ 10:25a · D✶♀ 1:54p · D✶♂ 8:48p · D△♄ 9:50p · D□♇ 10:20p	**14** — D→♓ 4:42a · ☿△♆ 1:09a	**15** — D✶♃ 4:59a · D→♈ 2:45p	**16** — Europe Day — D♂♂ 6:32a · D♂♀ 6:59a · D✶♀ 11:54a	**17** — D in ♈ — D♂♅ 5:11a · D✶♀ 9:10a · D△♄ 9:20a	**18** — D in ♈ — D□♀ 5:12a · D△♂ 10:33a · D→♈ 3:03a	**19** — Armed Forces Day · D in ♉
20 — Solar Eclipse New Moon 0♊21 4:47p · Sun enters Gemini — D△♃ 7:13a · ☉♂♅ 8:16a · D♂☉ 4:47p · D✶♇ 10:23p	**21** — Victoria Day — D✶♅ 7:13a · D□♀ 10:58p	**22** — D in ♊ — D▽♃ 3:51p	**23** — D→♋ 4:31a — D△☿ 10:43a · ☉□♀ 1:57p · D✶♂ 7:30p · D□♆ 10:34p	**24** — Ascension Day · D in ♋ — D✶♅ 2:40p · D△♇ 2:44p	**25** — D✶♆ 7:34a · D→♌ 3:11p — D□♀ 9:18a · D✶♂ 9:46p · D△♄ 11:32p	**26** — D in ♌
27 — Shavuot · Whit Sunday/Pentecost — D▽♃ 4:54p · D→♍ 11:06p	**28** — Memorial Day — D♂♆ 4:46a · D✶♅ 9:05a · D△☿ 3:16p · D□♀ 4:53p · D♂☉ 11:29p	**29** — D in ♍ — D▽♃ 10:50p	**30** — D→♎ 3:46a — D♂♃ 4:56p · D□☿ 5:20p · D✶♀ 6:54p · D△☉ 8:48p	**31** — D in ♎ — D→♎ 6:31p · D△♀ 5:44a · D□♆ 11:30a · D♂♄ 6:31p		

Legend

Moon goes void-of-course.
Moon enters next sign.
D✶☉ 1:41a — Daily aspects (when exact)
Sign or Direction changes

D✶☉ 5:35a
D→♋ 4:05p

Solar Eclipse New Moon 0♊21 4:47p
Sun enters Gemini
Sun aspects (when exact)

	APRIL 2012					
S	M	T	W	T	F	S
1	2	3	4	5	6	7
8	9	10	11	12	13	14
15	16	17	18	19	20	21
22	23	24	25	26	27	28
29	30					

	JUNE 2012					
S	M	T	W	T	F	S
					1	2
3	4	5	6	7	8	9
10	11	12	13	14	15	16
17	18	19	20	21	22	23
24	25	26	27	28	29	30

Pacific Daylight Saving Time

JUNE 2012

Day	☉	☿	♀	♂	♃	♄	♅	♆	♇	Mean Node
1	12Ⅱ	19Ⅱ	18R Ⅱ	15♍	28♉	23R♎	08♈	03♓	09R♑	05♐
2	13	21	18Ⅱ	16	28	23	08	03	09	05
3	14	23	17	16	28	23	08	03R	09	05
4	15	25	16	17	29	23	08	03	09	05
5	16	27	16	17	29	23	08	03	09	05
6	17	29	15	18	29	23	08	03	09	05
7	18	01♋	14	18	29	23	08	03	09	04
8	19	03	13	19	29	23	08	03	09	04
9	20	05	13	19	30	23	08	03	09	04
10	20	07	12	19	30	23	08	03	09	04
11	21	09	12	20	00Ⅱ	23	08	03	09	04
12	22	10	11	20	00	23	08	03	09	04
13	23	12	11	21	01	23	08	03	09	04
14	24	14	10	21	01	23	08	03	09	04
15	25	15	10	22	01	23	08	03	08	04
16	26	17	10	22	01	23	08	03	08	04
17	27	19	09	23	01	23	08	03	08	04
18	28	20	09	23	02	23	08	03	08	04
19	29	22	09	24	02	22D	08	03	08	04
20	00♋	23	09	24	02	22	08	03	08	04
21	01	25	09	25	03	22	08	03	08	04
22	02	26	07D	25	03	22	08	03	08	04
23	03	27	08	26	03	22	08	03	08	04
24	04	29	08	26	03	22	08	03	08	04
25	05	00♌	08	27	03	22	08	03	08	04
26	06	01	08	27	04	22	08	03	08	04
27	07	03	08	28	04	22	08	03	08	04
28	08	04	08	28	04	22	08	03	08	03
29	09	04	08	29	04	22	08	03	08	03
30	10	05	08	29	04	22	08	03	08	03

Above are rounded to nearest whole degree. Positions more than 29°30' round to 30° of one sign before 00° of the next sign. See pages 50–61 for a complete ephemeris.

June Planting Days
Above-ground crops: Best: 1, 2, 19, 20, 21, 29, 30. Good: 26, 27, 28
Root crops/perennials: Best: 10, 11 Good: 5, 6, 14, 15, 16

Planets Visible in the Morning Sky
Venus from the 13th and Jupiter. **Do not confuse** Venus with Jupiter late in the month; Venus is brighter.

Planets Visible in the Evening Sky
Mercury from the 4th, Mars, and Saturn.

GEMINI Ⅱ

May 20 to June 20 "I THINK"

A mutable, air sign with neutral polarity.
SYMBOL: the twins, Castor and Pollux.
COLORS: a variety—just about all! RULING PLANET: Mercury.
RULES: the nervous system, hands, shoulders, arms and lungs.
KEYWORDS: versatile, flexible, sociable, dualistic, curious, inquisitive

JUNE 2012

SUNDAY	MONDAY	TUESDAY	WEDNESDAY	THURSDAY	FRIDAY	SATURDAY
		MAY 2012 S M T W T F S 1 2 3 4 5 6 7 8 9 10 11 12 13 14 15 16 17 18 19 20 21 22 23 24 25 26 27 28 29 30 31 **JULY 2012** S M T W T F S 1 2 3 4 5 6 7 8 9 10 11 12 13 14 15 16 17 18 19 20 21 22 23 24 25 26 27 28 29 30 31	Moon goes void-of-course. Moon enters next sign. ☽v/c 3:53a ☽→♎ 10:15a First Qtr 5♎54 8:30p ☽☌♂ 3:53a ☽⚹☿ 11:40a ☽△♃ 4:10p ☽□☉ 8:30p ☽△♀ 11:16p Daily aspects (when exact) Sign or Direction changes		**1** ☽→♏ 5:31a GEMINI ☽△♆ 10:37a ☿☌♀ 1:32p ☽⚹♇ 7:55p	**2** ☽ in ♏ ☽⚹♂ 6:14a
3 ☽v/c 2:29a ☽→♐ 5:32a ☽☍♃ 2:29a ☽□♆ 10:34a ☽△♅ 6:09p ☿△♄ 7:38p	**4** ☽ in ♐ ☽v/c 10:08p **Lunar Eclipse** Full Moon 14♐14 4:12a ☽☍☉ 4:12a ☽□♂ 7:22a ☽☍♀ 8:02a ♆SR 2:05p ♀□♂ 5:29p ☽⚹♄ 6:23p ☽☍☿ 10:08p	**5** ☽→♑ 5:31a ☽⚹♆ 10:38a ☉☌♀ 6:10p ☽□♅ 6:31p ☽☌♇ 7:54p	**6** ☽ in ♑ ☽△♂ 9:33a ☽□♄ 7:29p	**7** ☽v/c 5:38a ☽→♒ 7:17a ☿→♋ 4:16a ☽△♃ 5:38a ☉□♂ 7:30p ☽⚹♅ 9:08p	**8** ☽ in ♒ ☽△♀ 7:49a ☽△☉ 3:35p ☿△♆ 6:50p ☽△♄ 11:35p	**9** ☽v/c 11:33a ☽→♓ 12:22p ☽□♃ 11:33a ☽☌♆ 6:10p ☽△☿ 10:11p
10 ☽ in ♓ ☽⚹♇ 4:34a ☽□♀ 12:16p	**11** ☽v/c 3:41a ☽→♈ 9:21p Last Qtr 20♓54 3:41a ☽☍♂ 0:16a ☽□☉ 3:41a ♃→♊ 10:22a ☿□♅ 10:42a ☿☍♇ 6:04p ☽⚹♃ 9:34p	**12** ☽ in ♈ ☽☌♅ 1:28p ☽□♇ 2:28p ☽□☿ 6:05p ☽⚹♀ 8:09p	**13** ☽ in ♈ ☽v/c 8:09p ☉△♄ 5:14a ☽☍♄ 6:55p ☽⚹☉ 8:09p	**14** ☽→♉ 9:22a Flag Day ☽⚹♆ 3:43p	**15** ☽ in ♉ ☽△♇ 2:53a ☽⚹☿ 5:00p	**16** ☽v/c 5:09a ☽→♊ 10:24p ☽△♂ 5:09a
17 ☽ in ♊ ☽☌♃ 0:58a ☽□♆ 4:43a ☽⚹♅ 3:09p ☽☌♀ 5:13p Father's Day	**18** ☽ in ♊ ☽□♂ 8:11p ☽△♄ 8:16p	**19** ☽v/c 8:02a ☽→♋ 10:34a New Moon 28♊43 8:02a ☽☌☉ 8:02a ☽△♆ 4:40p	**20** ☽ in ♋ ☽□♅ 2:57a ☽☍♇ 3:16a ☿□♄ 9:05a ☉→♋ 4:09p ♀⚹♅ 5:57p **Summer Solstice** **Sun enters Cancer**	**21** ☽v/c 9:48a ☽→♌ 8:47p ☿⚹♂ 3:15a ☽□♄ 6:58a ☽⚹♂ 9:18a ☽☌☿ 9:48a	**22** ☽ in ♌ CANCER ☽⚹♃ 1:19a ☽⚹♀ 11:50a ☽△♅ 12:38p	**23** ☽ in ♌ ☽v/c 3:26p ☽⚹♄ 3:26p ☉△♆ 8:55p
24 ☽→♍ 4:43a ♅□♇ 1:14a ☽□♃ 10:00a ☽☍♆ 10:16a ☽⚹☉ 11:18a ☽□♀ 6:32p ☽△♇ 7:54p	**25** ☽ in ♍ ♃□♆ 0:59a ♄SD 1:01a ☿→♌ 7:24p	**26** ☽v/c 3:53a ☽→♎ 10:15a First Qtr 5♎54 8:30p ☽☌♂ 3:53a ☽⚹☿ 11:40a ☽△♃ 4:10p ☽□☉ 8:30p ☽△♀ 11:16p	**27** ☽ in ♎ ☽□♇ 0:41a ☽☍♅ 0:53a ♀SD 8:07a	**28** ☽v/c 1:22a ☽→♏ 1:32p ☽☌♄ 1:22a ☽△♆ 6:34p ☽□☿ 7:13p	**29** ☽ in ♏ ☽△☉ 2:59a ☽⚹♇ 3:19a ☉☍♇ 8:00a ☿⚹♃ 8:39a ☉□♅ 1:11p	**30** ☽v/c 12:46p ☽→♐ 3:04p ☽⚹♂ 12:46p ☽□♆ 7:55p ☽☍♃ 10:05p

Pacific Daylight Saving Time

CANCER ♋

JULY 2012

Day	☉	☿	♀	♂	♃	♄	♅	♆	♇	Mean Node
1	11♋	06♌	08♊	29♍	04♊	23♎	08♈	03 R	08 R	03♐
2	11	07	08	30	05	23	08	03♓	08♑	03
3	12	08	08	00♎	05	23	09	03	08	03
4	13	09	08	01	05	23	09	03	08	03
5	14	09	09	01	05	23	09	03	08	03
6	15	10	09	02	06	23	09	03	08	03
7	16	11	09	02	06	23	09	03	08	03
8	17	11	10	03	06	23	09	03	08	03
9	18	12	10	03	06	23	09	03	08	03
10	19	12	11	04	06	23	09	03	08	03
11	20	12	11	05	07	23	09	03	08	03
12	21	12	12	05	07	23	09	03	08	03
13	22	12	12	06	07	23	09 R	03	08	03
14	23	13 R	13	06	07	23	09	03	08	03
15	24	13	13	07	07	23	09	03	08	03
16	25	12	14	07	08	23	09	03	08	03
17	26	12	14	08	08	23	09	03	08	02
18	27	12	15	08	08	23	09	03	08	02
19	28	12	16	09	08	23	09	03	08	02
20	29	11	16	10	08	23	09	03	08	02
21	30	11	17	10	08	23	08	03	08	02
22	01♌	10	18	11	09	23	08	03	08	02
23	02	10	18	11	09	23	08	03	08	02
24	02	09	19	12	09	23	08	03	08	02
25	03	08	20	12	09	24	08	02	08	02
26	04	07	20	13	09	24	08	02	08	02
27	05	07	21	14	10	24	08	02	08	02
28	06	06	22	14	10	24	08	02	08	02
29	07	05	23	15	10	24	08	02	08	02
30	08	05	24	15	10	24	08	02	07	02
31	09	04	24	16	10	24	08	02	07	02

Above are rounded to nearest whole degree. Positions more than 29°30' round to 30° of one sign before 00° of the next sign. See pages 50–61 for a complete ephemeris.

July Planting Days

Above-ground crops: Best: 26, 27 Good days: 24, 25, 30, 31
Root crops/perennials: Best: 7, 8, 17, 18 Good: 3, 4, 12, 13

Planets Visible in the Morning Sky

Venus and Jupiter. **Do not confuse** Venus with Jupiter early in the month; Venus is brighter.

Planets Visible in the Evening Sky

Mercury through the 21st, Mars, and Saturn.

CANCER ♋

June 20 to July 22 "I FEEL"

A cardinal, water sign of negative polarity.
SYMBOL: the crab.
RULES: the breasts, stomach, and solar plexus.
COLORS: silver and soft shades. RULING PLANET: the Moon.
KEYWORDS: fertile, domestic, nurturing, emotional, sensitive, evasive.

JULY 2012

SUNDAY	MONDAY	TUESDAY	WEDNESDAY	THURSDAY	FRIDAY	SATURDAY
1 ☽ in ♐ ☽△☿ 0:11a ☽☍♀ 3:42a ☽△♅ 4:52a Canada Day	**2** ☽v/c 3:21p ☽→♑ 3:51p ☽⚹♄ 4:08a ☽□♂ 3:21p ☽⚹♆ 8:39p	**3** ☽ in ♑ Full Moon 12♑14 11:52a ☽⚻♇ 5:11a ♂→♎ 5:32a ☽□♅ 5:45a ☽☍☉ 11:52a	**4** ☽v/c 5:25a ☽→♒ 5:26p ☽□♄ 5:25a ☿⚹♀ 6:27a ☿△♅ 10:54a ☽△♂ 6:49p ♀⚹♅ 7:36p U.S. Independence Day	**5** ☽ in ♒ ☽△♃ 2:12a ☽⚹♅ 7:53a ☽△♀ 8:08a ☽☍☿ 9:00a	**6** ☽v/c 8:48a ☽→♓ 9:29p ☽△♄ 8:48a	**7** ☽ in ♓ ☽☌♆ 2:40a ☽□♃ 7:40a ☽⚹♇ 12:04p ☽□♀ 2:29p
8 ☽ in ♓ ☽v/c 4:00a ☽△☉ 4:00a	**9** ☽→♈ 5:14a ☽☍♂ 11:41a ☽⚹♃ 5:06p ☽□♇ 8:44p ☽☌♅ 9:47p	**10** ☽ in ♈ Last Qtr 19♈11 6:48p ☽⚹♀ 1:18a ☽△☿ 3:59a ☽□☉ 6:48p	**11** ☽v/c 2:23a ☽→♉ 4:30p ☽☍♄ 2:23a ☽⚹♆ 10:10p	**12** ☽ in ♉ ☽△♇ 8:34a ☽□☿ 5:35p	**13** ☽ in ♉ ☽v/c 12:46p ♅SR 2:49a ☽⚹☉ 12:46p	**14** ☽→♊ 5:26a ☽□♆ 11:01a ☿⚹♀ 3:42p ☽△♂ 6:05p ☿SR 7:16p ☽⚻♃ 7:56p ☉□♄ 9:14p ☽⚹♅ 10:43p
15 ☽ in ♊ ☽⚹☿ 6:46a ☽☌♀ 7:30a	**16** ☽v/c 3:56a ☽→♋ 5:31p ☽△♄ 3:56a ☽△♆ 10:50p	**17** ☽ in ♋ ♂△♃ 5:40a ☽□♂ 8:34a ☽☍♇ 8:48a ☽□♅ 10:12a ♂□♇ 1:23p	**18** ☽ in ♋ ☽v/c 9:24p New Moon 26♋55 9:24p ☽□♄ 2:24p ♂☍♅ 7:56p ☽☌☉ 9:24p	**19** ☽→♌ 3:13a ☽⚹♃ 6:22p ☽△♅ 7:08p ☽⚹♂ 8:12p	**20** ☽ in ♌ ☽v/c 10:17p ☽⚻☿ 0:34a ☽⚹♀ 8:51a ☽⚹♄ 10:17p Ramadan begins	**21** ☽→♍ 10:24a ☽☍♆ 3:05p ♃⚹♅ 9:04p
22 ☽ in ♍ ☽v/c 5:44p ☽△♇ 0:14a ☽□♃ 1:44a ☉→♌ 3:01a ☿⚹♂ 3:55a ☽□♀ 5:44p **Sun enters Leo**	**23** ☽→♎ 3:38p LEO ☽⚹☉ 6:23p	**24** ☽ in ♎ ☽□♇ 4:59a ☽☍♅ 6:26a ☽△♃ 7:15a ☽⚹☿ 7:32a ☽☌♂ 12:09p ☿⚹♃ 12:15p	**25** ☽v/c 8:22a ☽→♏ 7:29p ☽△♀ 0:56a ☿△♅ 6:28a ☽☌♄ 8:22a ☽△♆ 11:46p	**26** ☽ in ♏ ☽v/c 8:38a First Qtr 3♏47 1:56a ☽□☉ 1:56a ☽⚹♇ 8:27a ☽□☿ 8:38a	**27** ☽→♐ 10:18p No exact aspects	**28** ☽ in ♐ ☽□♆ 2:25a ☽△☉ 8:16a ☽△☿ 8:48a ☽△♅ 12:28p ☉☌☿ 12:58p ☽☍♃ 2:37p ☽⚹♂ 10:23p
29 ☽ in ♐ ☽v/c 2:01p ☽☍♀ 12:07p ☽⚹♄ 2:01p	**30** ☽→♑ 0:29a ☽⚹♆ 4:31a ☽⚻♇ 1:03p ☽□♅ 2:34p ☉△♅ 10:22p	**31** ☽ in ♑ ☽v/c 4:30p ♀△♄ 0:40a ☽□♂ 2:43a ☽□♄ 4:30p				

JULY 2012

JUNE 2012

S	M	T	W	T	F	S
					1	2
3	4	5	6	7	8	9
10	11	12	13	14	15	16
17	18	19	20	21	22	23
24	25	26	27	28	29	30

AUGUST 2012

S	M	T	W	T	F	S
			1	2	3	4
5	6	7	8	9	10	11
12	13	14	15	16	17	18
19	20	21	22	23	24	25
26	27	28	29	30	31	

Moon goes void-of-course.
Moon enters next sign.
☽v/c 0:40a
☽→♓ 5:24a
Last Qtr 3♓16 11:52a
☽⚹♃ 0:40a
☽☌♆ 7:11a
☽□☉ 11:52a
☽⚹♇ 7:19p
☉⚹♅ 11:48p
Daily aspects (when exact)
Sign or Direction changes

Pacific Daylight Saving Time

Day	☉	☿	♀	♂	♃	♄	♅	♆	♇	Mean Node
1	10♌	03R♌	25♊	17♎	10♊	24♏	08♈	02R♓	07R♑	02♐
2	11	03R♌	26	17	10	24	08	02♓	07	02
3	12	02	27	18	11	24	08	02	07	02
4	13	02	28	18	11	24	08	02	07	01
5	14	02	29	19	11	24	08	02	07	01
6	15	01	00♋	20	12	24	08	02	07	01
7	16	01D	01	20	12	24	08	02	07	01
8	17	01	03	21	12	24	08	02	07	01
9	18	01	04	21	12	24	08	02	07	01
10	19	02	05	22	13	24	08	02	07	01
11	20	02	06	23	13	25	08	02	07	01
12	21	03	07	23	13	25	08	02	07	01
13	22	04	09	24	13	25	08	02	07	01
14	23	05	10	25	13	25	08	02	07	00
15	24	06	11	26	14	25	08	02	07	00
16	25	07	13	26	14	25	08	02	07	00
17	26	08	14	27	14	26	08	02	07	00
18	27	09	15	28	14	26	08	02	07	00
19	28	11	16	00♏	14	26	08	02	07	00
20	29	12	18	01	14	26	08	02	07	00
21	00♍	14	19	02	14	26	08	02	07	00
22	00♍	15	20	03	14	26	08	02	07	00
23	02	17	22	03	14	26	08	02	07	00
24	03	19	23	04	14	26	08	02	07	00
25	04	00♍	24	05	15	26	08	02	07	00
26	04	20	26	04	14	26	08	02	07	00
27	05	04	20	03	14	26	08	02	07	00
28	06	24	21	04	14	26	08	02	07	00
29	07	26	22	04	14	26	08	02	07	00
30	08	28	23	05	14	26	08	02	07	00
31	09♍	00♍	24	05	15	26	08	02	07	00

Above are rounded to nearest whole degree. Positions more than 29° 39' round to 30° of one sign before 00° of the next sign. See pages 50–61 for a complete ephemeris.

August Planting Days
Above-ground crops: Best: 22, 23   Good days: 20, 21, 26, 27
Root crops/perennials: Best: 3, 4, 5, 13, 14, 31   Good: 8, 9, 10

Planets Visible in the Morning Sky
Mercury from the 6th, Venus, and Jupiter.
Planets Visible in the Evening Sky
Mars and Saturn. **Do not confuse** Mars with Saturn mid-month;
Saturn is brighter.

LEO ♌
July 22 to August 22   "I WILL"

A fixed, fire sign of positive polarity.
SYMBOL: the majestic lion.
RULING PLANET: the Sun.
KEYWORDS: leadership
COLORS: gold and scarlet.
RULES: the heart and spine.

AUGUST 2012

JULY 2012

S	M	T	W	T	F	S
1	2	3	4	5	6	7
8	9	10	11	12	13	14
15	16	17	18	19	20	21
22	23	24	25	26	27	28
29	30	31				

SEPTEMBER 2012

S	M	T	W	T	F	S
						1
2	3	4	5	6	7	8
9	10	11	12	13	14	15
16	17	18	19	20	21	22
23/30	24	25	26	27	28	29

			Full Moon 10♒15 8:27p ☽→♒ 2:56a ☽☍☿ 8:58a ☽✶♅ 5:15p ☽☍☉ 8:27p ☽△♃ 8:50p	**2** ☽ in ♒ ☉✶♃ 2:56a ☽△♂ 8:07a ☽△♄ 8:19p	**3** ☽v/c 0:24a ☽→♓ 6:58a ☽△♀ 0:24a ☽☌♆ 11:04a ☽✶♇ 8:16p	**4** ☽ in ♓ ☽□♃ 2:27a
5 ☽v/c 10:56a ☽→♈ 1:59p ☽□♀ 10:56a ☽△☿ 5:11p	**6** ☽ in ♈ ☽□♇ 4:04a ☽☌♅ 5:51a ☽✶♃ 11:29a ☽△☉ 6:45p	**7** ☽ in ♈ ☽v/c 1:04p ☽☍♂ 4:27a ♀→♋ 6:43a ☽☍♄ 1:04p ☿SD 10:40p	**8** ☽→♉ 0:28a ☽✶♀ 1:54a ☽□☿ 3:20a ☽✶♆ 4:50a ☽△♇ 3:12p	Last Qtr 17♉34 11:55a ☽ in ♉ ☽v/c 11:55a ☽□☉ 11:55a ♀△♆ 3:36p	**10** ☽→♊ 1:11p ☽✶☿ 4:58p ☽□♆ 5:29p	**11** ☽ in ♊ ☽✶♅ 5:50a ☽☌♃ 1:32p
12 ☽ in ♊ ☽v/c 2:49p ☽✶☉ 6:01a ☽△♂ 11:55a ☽△♄ 2:49p Perseids meteors	**13** ☽→♋ 1:28a ☽△♆ 5:30a ☽☌♀ 12:45p ☽☍♇ 3:41p ☽□♅ 5:26p	**14** ☽ in ♋ No exact aspects	**15** ☽v/c 1:21a ☽→♌ 11:05a ☽□♂ 1:15a ☽□♄ 1:21a ♀☍♇ 2:09a ♂☌♄ 3:37a ☽☌☿ 8:24p ♀□♅ 11:49p	**16** ☽ in ♌ ☽△♅ 2:04a ☽✶♃ 10:32a	New Moon 25♌08 8:54a ☽v/c 10:55a ☽→♍ 5:33p ☉✶♄ 5:05a ☽✶♄ 8:39a ☽☌☉ 8:54a ☽✶♂ 10:55a ☽☍♆ 8:57p	**18** ☽ in ♍ ☽v/c 4:26p ☽△♇ 6:13a ☽✶♀ 12:05p ☽□♃ 4:26p ☿△♅ 4:30p
19 ☽→♎ 9:45p No exact aspects	**20** ☽ in ♎ ☽□♇ 10:00a ☽☍♅ 11:25a ☉✶♂ 2:47p ☽✶☿ 3:53p ☽□♀ 7:42p ☽△♃ 8:32p	**21** ☽ in ♎ ☽☌♄ 5:00p ☽☌♂ 11:24p	**22** ☽v/c 0:13a ☽→♏ 0:54a ☽✶☉ 0:13a ☽△♆ 3:58a ☉→♍ 10:07a ☽✶♇ 12:59p ☿✶♃ 3:57p **Sun enters Virgo**	**23** ☽ in ♏ ☽v/c 2:34a ☽□☿ 0:54a ☽△♀ 2:34a ♂→♏ 8:24a	First Qtr 1♐48 6:54a ☽→♐ 3:50a ☉☍♆ 5:33a ☽□♆ 6:48a ☽□☉ 6:54a ☽△♅ 5:11p	**25** ☽ in ♐ ☽v/c 11:39p ☽☍♃ 3:25a ☽△☿ 10:44a ☽✶♄ 11:39p ♂△♆ 11:55p
26 ☽→♑ 6:58a ☽✶♆ 9:52a ☽✶♂ 10:21a ☽△☉ 1:50p ☽☌♇ 7:05p ☽□♅ 8:19p Women's Equality Day	**27** ☽ in ♑ ☽☍♀ 5:02p	**28** ☽v/c 3:33a ☽→♒ 10:38a ☽□♄ 3:33a ☽□♂ 4:37p	**29** ☽ in ♒ ☽✶♅ 0:05a ☽△♃ 11:44a ☉△♇ 5:20p ☿✶♄ 6:25p	**30** ☽v/c 10:48a ☽→♓ 3:31p ☽△♄ 8:34a ☽☍☿ 10:48a ☽☌♆ 6:20p	**Blue Moon** Full Moon 8♓34 6:58a ☽ in ♓ ☽△♂ 0:25a ☽✶♇ 4:11a ☽☍☉ 6:58a ☽□♃ 5:58p ☿→♍ 7:32p	Moon goes void-of-course, Moon enters next sign. ☽v/c 10:55a ☽→♍ 5:33p New Moon 25♌08 8:54a ☉✶♄ 5:05a ☽✶♄ 8:39a ☽☌☉ 8:54a ☽✶♂ 10:55a ☽☍♆ 8:57p Daily aspects (when exact) Sign or Direction changes

Pacific Daylight Saving Time

Day	☉	☿	♀	♂	♃	♄	♅	♆	♇	Mean Node
1	10♍	02♍R	25♌	06♍	15♊	26♎	08♈R	02♓R	07♑R	30♏
2	11	04	26	07	15	26	08	01	07	30
3	12	06	27	08	15	27	08	01	07	30
4	13	08	28	09	15	27	07	01	07	30
5	14	10	29	09	15	27	07	01	07	30
6	15	11	00♍	10	15	27	07	01	07	30
7	16	13	01	11	15	27	07	01	07	30
8	17	15	03	12	15	27	07	01	07	29
9	18	17	04	13	16	27	07	01	07	29
10	19	19	05	14	16	28	07	01	07♑D	29
11	20	21	06	15	16	28	07	01	07	29
12	21	23	08	16	16	28	07	01	07	29
13	22	25	09	17	16	28	07	01	07	29
14	23	26	10	18	16	28	07	01	07	29
15	24	28	11	19	16	29	07	01	07	29
16	25	00♎D	13	20	16	29	07	01	07	29
17	26	02	14	21	16	29	07	01	07	29
18	27	04	15	22	16	29	07	01	07	29
19	28	05	16	23	16	29	07	01	07	29
20	29	07	18	23	16	29	07	01	07	29
21	00♎	09	19	24	16	29	07	01	07	29
22	01	10	20	25	16	29	07	01	07	29
23	02	12	21	25	16	29	07	01	07	29
24	03	14	23	26	16	29	07	01	07	29
25	04	15	24	27	16	29	07	01	07	29
26	05	17	25	28	16	29	07	01	07	29
27	06	19	26	28	16	29	07	01	07	29
28	07	20	27	29	16	29	06	01	07	29
29	08	22	29	00♎	16	29	06	01	07	29
30	09	23	00♎	01	16	29	06	01	07	28

Above are rounded to nearest whole degree. Positions more than 29°30' round to 30° of one sign before 00° of the next sign. See pages 50–61 for a complete ephemeris.

September Planting Days
Above-ground crops: Best: 18, 19, 27, 28   Good: 16, 17, 23, 24
Root crops/perennials: Best: 1, 9, 10, 11   Good days: 4, 5, 6

Planets Visible in the Morning Sky
  Mercury through the 1st, Venus, and Jupiter.
Planets Visible in the Evening Sky
  Mercury from the 22nd, Mars, and Saturn.

VIRGO ♍
August 22 to September 22 "I ANALYZE"
A mutable, earth sign of negative polarity.
SYMBOL: a virgin with a shaft of wheat.
COLORS: gray and navy blue.   RULING PLANET: Mercury.
RULES: the intestinal tract and powers of assimilation.

SEPTEMBER 2012

			Moon enters next sign. First Qtr 0♑12 12:41p ☽v/c 9:45a ☽→♑ 12:20p ☉→♎ 7:49a ☽✶♄ 9:45a ☽□☉ 12:41p ☽✶♆ 2:02p **Sun enters Libra Autumnal Equinox** Daily aspects (when exact) Sign or Direction changes	AUGUST 2012 S M T W T F S 1 2 3 4 5 6 7 8 9 10 11 12 13 14 15 16 17 18 19 20 21 22 23 24 25 26 27 28 29 30 31 OCTOBER 2012 S M T W T F S 1 2 3 4 5 6 7 8 9 10 11 12 13 14 15 16 17 18 19 20 21 22 23 24 25 26 27 28 29 30 31		**1** ☽v/c 1:02p ☽→♈ 10:37p ☽△♀ 1:02p ☿☍♆ 2:17p
2 ☽ in ♈ VIRGO ☽□♇ 11:55a ☽☌♅ 12:59p	**3** ☽ in ♈ ♀□♄ 0:46a ☽✶♃ 2:57a Labor Day ♂✶♇ 4:02a	**4** ☽v/c 4:06a ☽→♉ 8:41a ☽☍♄ 1:54a ☽□♀ 4:06a ☿△♇ 9:46a ☽✶♆ 11:33a ☽△♇ 10:38p	**5** ☽ in ♉ ☽v/c 11:54a ☿✶♂ 1:06a ☽☍♂ 1:08a ☽△☿ 1:08a ☽△☉ 11:54a	**6** ☽→♊ 9:10p ♀→♌ 7:48a ☽✶♀ 10:31p ☽□♆ 11:58p	**7** ☽ in ♊ ☉□♃ 3:15a ☽✶♅ 12:12p	☽ in ♊ Last Qtr 16♊17 6:15a ☽□☿ 1:49a ☽●♃ 4:13a ☽□☉ 6:15a ☿□♃ 5:14p
9 ☽v/c 3:59a ☽→♋ 9:49a ☽△♄ 3:59a ☽△♆ 12:26p ☽☍♇ 11:38p Grandparents' Day	**10** ☽ in ♋ ☽□♅ 0:17a ☉☌☿ 5:44a ☽△♂ 9:05a ☽✶☉ 10:54p	**11** ☽v/c 2:58p ☽→♌ 8:01p ☽✶☿ 0:22a ☽□♄ 2:58p	**12** ☽ in ♌ ☽☌♀ 8:16a ☽△♅ 9:27a ☽□♂ 8:54p ♀△♅ 9:46p	**13** ☽ in ♌ ☽v/c 10:14p ☽✶♃ 0:53a ☽✶♄ 10:14p	**14** ☽→♍ 2:31a ☽☍♆ 4:36a ☽△♇ 2:39p	☽ in ♍ New Moon 23♍37 7:11p ☽✶♂ 4:33a ☽□♃ 5:52a ☽☌☉ 7:11p
16 ☽v/c 4:26a ☽→♎ 5:55a ☽☌☿ 4:26a ☿→♎ 4:22p ☽□♇ 5:33p ☽☍♅ 5:42p	**17** ☽ in ♎ ☽✶♀ 1:39a ☽△♃ 8:27a ♇SD 10:05p Rosh Hashanah begins	**18** ☽v/c 4:30a ☽→♏ 7:46a ☽☌♄ 4:30a ☽△♆ 9:34a ☽✶♇ 7:16p ♅□♇ 11:55p	**19** ☽ in ♏ ☽□♀ 7:29a ☽●♂ 1:33p	**20** ☽v/c 6:11a ☽→♐ 9:34a ☽✶☉ 6:11a ☽□♆ 11:18a ☿☍♅ 3:24p ☿□♇ 4:19p ♀✶♃ 8:45p ☽△♅ 9:06p ☽✶☿ 9:53p	**21** ☽ in ♐ ☽☍♃ 12:41p ☽△♀ 2:01p Int'l Day of Peace	First Qtr 0♑12 12:41p ☽v/c 9:45a ☽→♑ 12:20p ☉→♎ 7:49a ☽✶♄ 9:45a ☽□☉ 12:41p ☽✶♆ 2:02p **Sun enters Libra Autumnal Equinox**
23 ☽ in ♑ ☽□♅ 0:02a ☽●♇ 0:19a ☽□☿ 8:02a **30** ☽ in ♈ ☽✶♃ 1:40p	**24** ☽v/c 2:19p ☽→♒ 4:32p LIBRA ☽✶♂ 0:49a ☽□♄ 2:19p ☽△☉ 8:57p	**25** ☽ in ♒ ☽✶♅ 4:26a ☽△☿ 8:13p ☽△♃ 9:31p	**26** ☽v/c 8:33p ☽→♓ 10:24p ☿△♃ 7:09a ☽☍♀ 8:27a ☽□♂ 9:05a Yom Kippur ☽△♄ 8:33p	**27** ☽ in ♓ ☽☌♆ 0:01a ♀□♂ 1:50a ☽✶♇ 11:11a	**28** ☽ in ♓ ☽v/c 7:35p ☽□♃ 4:30a ☽△♂ 7:35p American Indian Day	☽→♈ 6:14a **Harvest Moon** Full Moon 7♈22 8:19p ☉☍♅ 0:16a ☉□♇ 10:54a ☽☌♅ 6:40p ☽□♇ 7:34p ☽☍☉ 8:19p

Pacific Daylight Saving Time

LIBRA ♎

Day	☉	☿	♀	♂	♃	♄	♅	♆	♇	Mean Node
1	09♎	25♎	28♌	26♏	16♊	30♎	06♈R	01♓R	07♑R	28♏
2	10	26	29	27	16	30	06T	01T	07	28
3	11	28	01♍	28	16	30	06	01	07	28
4	12	29♎	02	28	16	30	06	01	07	28
5	13	01♏	03	29	16R	00♏	06	01	07	28
6	14	02	04	00♐	16	00	06	01	07	28
7	15	04	05	01	16	00	06	01	07	28
8	16	05	06	02	16	00	06	01	07	28
9	17	07	08	02	16	00	06	01	07	28
10	18	08	09	03	16	01	06	01	07	28
11	19	10	10	04	16	01	06	01	07	28
12	20	11	11	05	16	01	06	00	07	27
13	21	12	13	05	16	01	06	00	07	27
14	22	14	14	06	16	01	06	00	07	27
15	23	15	15	07	16	02	06	00	07	27
16	24	17	16	08	16	02	05	00	07	27
17	25	19	17	09	16	02	05	00	07	27
18	26	20	19	09	16	02	05	00	07	27
19	27	21	20	10	16	02	05	00	07	27
20	28	23	21	11	16	03	05	00	07	27
21	29♎	29♏	22	11	16	03	05	00	07	27
22	00♏	00♏	23	12	16	03	05	00	07	27
23	01	01	25	13	16	03	05	00	07	27
24	02	03	26	14	15	03	05	00	07	27
25	03	04	27	14	15	03	05	00	07	27
26	04	05	28	15	15	03	05	00	07	27
27	05	06	29♍	16	15	03	05	00	07	27
28	06	06	01♎	16	15	03	05	00	07	27
29	07	07	02	17	15	03	05	00	07	27
30	08	01♐	03	17	15	03	05	00	07	27
31	09	02	04	18	15	03	05	00	07	27

Above are rounded to nearest whole degree. Positions more than 29°30' round to 30° of one sign before 00° of the next sign. See pages 50–61 for a complete ephemeris.

October Planting Days
Above-ground crops: Best: 16, 17, 24, 25, 26   Good: 15, 20, 21
Root crops/perennials: Best: 7, 8   Good days: 2, 3, 14, 29, 30

Planets Visible in the Morning Sky: Venus and Jupiter.
Planets Visible in the Evening Sky
Mercury, Mars, and Saturn through the 8th. **Do not confuse**
Mercury with Saturn early in the month; Mercury is brighter.

LIBRA ♎
September 22 to October 22 "I BALANCE"
A cardinal, air sign of positive polarity.
SYMBOL: the balance (scales of justice) or the Sun on the horizon
as the balance between night and day.

COLORS: lighter blues, pink, and soft rose.

OCTOBER 2012

SEPTEMBER 2012

S	M	T	W	T	F	S
						1
2	3	4	5	6	7	8
9	10	11	12	13	14	15
16	17	18	19	20	21	22
23	24	25	26	27	28	29
30						

NOVEMBER 2012

S	M	T	W	T	F	S
				1	2	3
4	5	6	7	8	9	10
11	12	13	14	15	16	17
18	19	20	21	22	23	24
25	26	27	28	29	30	

SUNDAY	MONDAY	TUESDAY	WEDNESDAY	THURSDAY	FRIDAY	SATURDAY
	1 ☽v/c 3:32p ☽→♉ 4:26p ☽☍☿ 4:36a ☽△♀ 1:06p ☽☍♄ 3:32p ☽✶♆ 6:00p Sukkoth	**2** ☽ in ♉ LIBRA ☽△♇ 6:22a ♀✶♄ 5:07p ♀→♍ 11:59p	**3** ☽ in ♉ ♀☍♆ 3:28p	**4** ☽v/c 0:44a ☽→♊ 4:47a ☽☍♂ 0:44a ☽□♆ 6:17a ♃SR 6:18a ☽□♀ 7:56a ☽✶♅ 5:39p	**5** ☽ in ♊ ☽v/c 2:08p ☿☌♄ 2:44a ☿→♏ 3:35a ☽△☉ 6:41a ♄→♏ 1:33p ☽⚻♃ 2:08p ☿△♆ 3:07p	**6** ☽→♋ 5:45p ☽△♄ 6:02p ☽△♆ 7:09p ♂→♐ 8:21p ☽△☿ 11:09p
7 ☽ in ♋ ☽✶♀ 3:29a ☽□♅ 6:15a ☽☍♇ 7:55a ♂□♆ 7:12p	**8** ☽ in ♋ ☽v/c 0:33a Last Qtr 15♋26 0:33a ☽□☉ 0:33a ☉△♃ 10:52p Columbus Day Thanksgiving (Canada)	**9** ☽→♌ 4:55a ♀△♇ 1:03a ☽□♄ 5:45a ☽△♂ 8:18a ☽△♅ 4:34p ☽□☿ 5:36p	**10** ☽ in ♌ ☽v/c 2:40p ☿✶♇ 0:31a ☽✶♃ 11:36a ☽✶☉ 2:40p ♄△♆ 7:42p	**11** ☽→♍ 12:23p ☽☍♆ 1:29p ☽✶♄ 1:39p ☽□♂ 6:36p	**12** ☽ in ♍ ☽v/c 4:48p ☽△♇ 0:56a ☽✶☿ 6:23a ☽☌♀ 7:36a ☽□♃ 4:48p	**13** ☽→♎ 4:02p No exact aspects
14 ☽ in ♎ ☽✶♂ 0:31a ☽☍♅ 1:55a ☽□♇ 3:52a ☽△♃ 6:44p	**15** ☽v/c 5:03a ☽→♏ 5:06p New Moon 22♎32 5:03a ♂△♅ 3:34a ☽☌☉ 5:03a ☽△♆ 6:00p ☽☌♄ 7:04p	**16** ☽ in ♏ ☽v/c 7:23p ☽✶♇ 4:38a ☿✶♀ 5:32a ♀□♃ 4:34p ☽✶♀ 7:16p ☽⚻☿ 7:23p	**17** ☽→♐ 5:26p ☽□♆ 6:17p	**18** ☽ in ♐ ☽⚼♅ 2:50a ☽☌♂ 6:41a ☽☍♃ 7:32p	**19** ☽v/c 1:27p ☽→♑ 6:41p ☽□♀ 0:15a ☽✶☉ 1:27p ☽✶♆ 7:31p ☽✶♄ 9:33p	**20** ☽ in ♑ ☽□♅ 4:18a ☽⚻♇ 6:49a
21 ☽v/c 8:32p ☽→♒ 10:02p First Qtr 29♑09 8:32p ☽△♀ 7:29a ☽✶☿ 8:05a ☽□☉ 8:32p Orionids meteor showers	**22** ☽ in ♒ ☽□♄ 1:30a ☽✶♅ 8:00a ☉→♏ 5:14p ☽✶♂ 6:16p **Sun enters Scorpio**	**23** ☽ in ♒ ☽v/c 6:27p ☽△♃ 2:06a ☉△♆ 4:15a ☽□☿ 6:27p	**24** ☽→♓ 4:00a ☽☌♆ 4:50a ☽△☉ 6:53a ☽△♄ 8:09a ☽✶♇ 5:31p United Nations Day	**25** ☽ in ♓ SCORPIO ☉☌♄ 1:32a ☽□♂ 4:33a ☽□♃ 9:09a ☿✶♀ 10:11a	**26** ☽v/c 8:04a ☽→♈ 12:31p ☽△☿ 7:44a ☽☍♀ 8:04a ☽☌♅ 11:06p	**27** ☽ in ♈ ☽v/c 6:32p ☽□♇ 2:42a ☽△♂ 5:44p ☽✶♃ 6:32p
28 ☽→♉ 11:15p ♂☍♃ 5:56a ♀→♎ 6:04a ☿→♐ 11:18p	**29** ☽ in ♉ ☽v/c 2:01p Full Moon 6♉48 12:49p ☽✶♆ 0:04a ☽☍♄ 4:55a ☿□♆ 10:41a ☽☍☉ 12:49p ☽△♇ 2:01p	**30** ☽v/c in ♉ ☉✶♇ 3:28a	**31** ☽→♊ 11:40a ☽□♆ 12:28p ☽☍☿ 3:55p ☽△♀ 8:33p ☽✶♅ 10:30p Halloween	OCTOBER 2012		Moon goes void-of-course, Moon enters next sign. New Moon 22♎32 5:03a ☽v/c 5:03a ☽→♏ 5:06p ♂△♅ 3:34a ☽☌☉ 5:03a ☽△♆ 6:00p ☽☌♄ 7:04p Daily aspects (when exact) Sign or Direction changes

Pacific Daylight Saving Time

NOVEMBER 2012

Day	☉	☿	♀	♂	♃	♄	⛢	♆	♇	Mean Node
1	10♏	03♐	05♎	19♐	15♉R	03♏	05♈R	00♈R	07♈R	27♏R
2	11	03	07	19	15	03	05♊	00♓	07	27
3	12	04	08	20	15	04	05	00	08	27
4	13	04	09	21	15	04	05	00	08	27
5	14	04	11	22	15	04	05	00	08	27
6	15	04R	12	23	14	04	05	00	08	26
7	16	04	13	23	14	04	05	00	08	26
8	17	04	14	24	14	04	05	00	08	26
9	18	03	15	25	14	04	05	00	08	26
10	19	03	16	25	14	04	05	00	08	26
11	20	02	18	26	14	04	05	00	08	26
12	21	01	19	27	14	04	05	00	08	26
13	22	00	20	28	14	05	05	00	08	26
14	23	29♏	21	28	14	05	05	00	08	26
15	24	28	22	29	14	05	05	00	08	26
16	25	27	24	00♐	13	05	05	00	08	26
17	26	25	25	01	13	05	05	00	08	26
18	27	24	26	01	13	05	05	00	08	26
19	28	23	27	02	13	06	05	00	08	26
20	29	22	29	03	13	06	05	00	08	25
21	00♐R	20	00♏	04	13	06	05	00D	08	25
22	01	20	01	04	13	06	05	00	08	25
23	02	19	02	05	12	06	05	00	08	25
24	03	19	03	06	12	06	05	00	08	25
25	04	18	05	07	12	06	05	00	08	26
26	05	18D	06	08	12	06	05	00	08	25
27	06	18	07	08	12	07	05	00	08	25
28	07	19	08	09	12	07	05	00	08	25
29	08	19	10	10	12	07	05	00	08	25
30	09	20	11	11	12	07	05	00	08	25

Above are rounded to nearest whole degree. Positions more than 29°30' round to 30°
of one sign before 00° of the next sign. See pages 50–61 for a complete ephemeris.

November Planting Days
Above-ground crops: Best: 20, 21, 22   Good: 16, 17, 25, 26, 27
Root crops/perennials: Best: 3, 4, 12, 13, 30   Good: 10, 11
Planets Visible in the Morning Sky
Mercury from the 24th, Venus, Jupiter, and Saturn from the 12th.
Do not confuse Venus with Saturn late month; Venus is brighter.
Planets Visible in the Evening Sky
Mercury through the 12th and Mars.

SCORPIO ♏, October 22 to November 21 "I CREATE"
A fixed, water sign of negative polarity.
SYMBOLS: the scorpion, eagle, and phoenix (the mythical bird
consumed in the solar fire and arising again from its own ashes).
COLORS: deep reds.   RULES: the generative system.
RULING PLANETS: Mars and Pluto.
KEYWORDS: resourceful, secretive, passionate, intense, transformative.

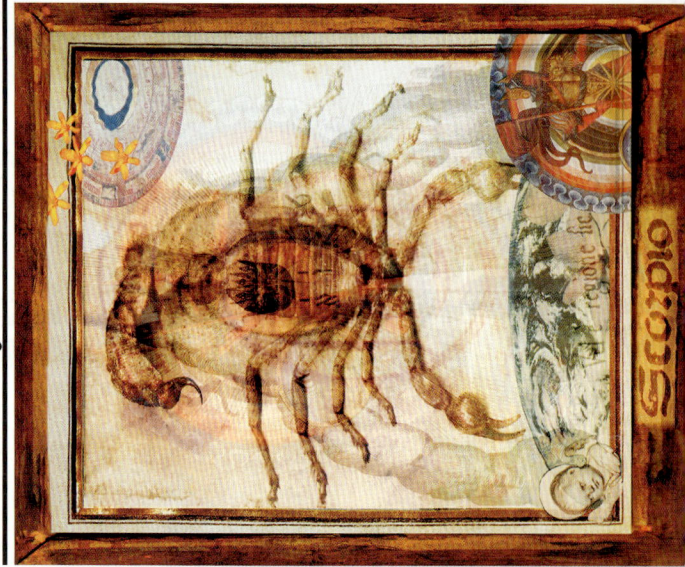

SUNDAY	MONDAY	TUESDAY	WEDNESDAY	THURSDAY	FRIDAY	SATURDAY
NOVEMBER 2012			OCTOBER 2012 S M T W T F S 1 2 3 4 5 6 7 8 9 10 11 12 13 14 15 16 17 18 19 20 21 22 23 24 25 26 27 28 29 30 31 DECEMBER 2012 S M T W T F S 1 2 3 4 5 6 7 8 9 10 11 12 13 14 15 16 17 18 19 20 21 22 23 24 25 26 27 28 29 30 31	**1** ☽ in ♊ SCORPIO ♀☍♅ 3:06p ☽☌♃ 6:18p All Saints Day	**2** ☽ in ♊ ☽v/c 2:21a ☽☍♂ 2:21a	**3** ☽→♋ 0:43a ☽△♆ 1:30a ☽△♄ 7:43a ♀□♇ 10:26a ☽□♅ 11:20a ☽☍♇ 3:54p ☽□♀ 4:31p
4 ☽ in ♋ ☽v/c 1:37a ☽△☉ 1:37a Daylight Saving ends	**5** ☽→♌ 11:39a ☽□♄ 6:58p ☽△☿ 7:57p ☽△♅ 9:44p	**6** ☽ in ♌ Last Qtr 15♌00 4:36p ☽⚹♀ 9:14a ☿SR 3:04p ☽⚹♃ 3:45p ☽□☉ 4:36p Election Day	**7** ☽v/c 7:27a ☽→♍ 8:35p ☽△♂ 7:27a ☽☍♆ 9:15p	**8** ☽ in ♍ ☽⚹♄ 3:57a ☽□☿ 4:06a ☽△♇ 10:25a ☽□♃ 10:23p ♀△♃ 11:26p	**9** ☽ in ♍ ☽v/c 4:27p ☽⚹☉ 3:57a ☽□♂ 4:27p	**10** ☽→♎ 1:35a ☽⚹☿ 7:06a ☽☍♅ 10:08a ☽□♇ 2:33p ♆SD 11:53p
11 ☽ in ♎ ☽v/c 9:13p ☽△♃ 1:13a ☽☌♀ 6:13a ☽⚹♂ 9:13p Veterans Day	**12** ☽→♏ 3:10a ☽△♆ 3:45a ☽☌♄ 10:28a ☽⚹♇ 3:34p	**13** ☽ in ♏ Solar Eclipse New Moon 21♏57 2:08p ☽☌☉ 2:08p ☿□♆ 4:02p ☿→♏ 11:43p	**14** ☽v/c 2:39a ☽→♐ 2:52a ☽☌☿ 2:39a ☽□♆ 3:27a ☽△♅ 10:42a	**15** ☽ in ♐ ☽☍♃ 0:25a ☽⚹♀ 2:29p	**16** ☽v/c 1:44a ☽→♑ 2:35a ☽☌♂ 1:44a ☽⚹♆ 3:11a ☽□♅ 10:32a ☽⚹♄ 10:42a ☽☌♇ 3:18p ♂→♑ 6:36p Leonids meteors	**17** ☽ in ♑ ☽v/c 9:54p ♂⚹♆ 6:23a ☉☌☿ 7:47a ☽⚹☿ 7:46p ☽□♀ 8:03p ☽⚹☉ 9:54p
18 ☽→♒ 4:10a ☽⚹♅ 12:29p ☽□♄ 1:10p	**19** ☽ in ♒ ☽△♃ 2:47a ☽□☿ 7:22p	**20** ☽v/c 6:31a ☽→♓ 8:55a First Qtr 28♒41 6:31a ☽△♀ 5:35a ☽□☉ 6:31a ☽☌♆ 9:38a ☽⚹♂ 2:11p ☽△♄ 7:01p ☽⚹♇ 11:31p	**21** ☽ in ♓ ☽v/c 10:32p ☽□♃ 8:34a ☉→♐ 1:50p ♀→♏ 5:20p ☽△☿ 10:32p ☉□♆ 11:13p **Sun enters Sagittarius**	**22** ☽→♈ 5:12p ♀△♆ 1:00a ☽△☉ 7:37p Thanksgiving Day	**23** ☽ in ♈ ☽v/c 5:34p ♂□♅ 2:06a ☽☌♅ 2:27a ☽□♂ 2:29a ☽□♇ 8:47a ☽⚹♃ 5:34p	**24** ☽v/c in ♈ *get Calendars for 2013* ♂⚹♄ 2:53p
25 ☽→♉ 4:18a SAGITTARIUS ☽⚹♆ 5:09a ☽☍♀ 1:53p ☽☍♄ 4:30p ☽△♂ 6:00p ☽△♇ 8:36p	**26** ☽ in ♉ ☽v/c 4:57p ☉△♅ 6:16a ☿SD 2:48p ☽☍☿ 4:57p ♀☌♄ 5:19p	**27** ☽→♊ 4:58p ♂☌♇ 12:14p ☽□♆ 5:53p	**28** ☽ in ♊ ☽v/c 5:04p Lunar Eclipse Full Moon 6♊47 6:46a ☽⚹♅ 2:33a ☽☍☉ 6:46a ♀⚹♇ 8:01a ☽☌♃ 5:04p	**29** ☽v/c in ♊ ♀⚹♂ 2:34p	**30** ☽→♋ 5:55a ☽△♆ 6:52a ☽□♅ 3:22p ☽△♄ 7:18p ☽☍♇ 10:36p	Moon goes void-of-course, Moon enters next sign. ☽v/c 6:31a ☽→♓ 8:55a First Qtr 28♒41 6:31a ☽△♀ 5:35a ☽□☉ 6:31a ☽☌♆ 9:38a ☽⚹♂ 2:11p ☽△♄ 7:01p ☽⚹♇ 11:31p Daily aspects (when exact) Sign or Direction changes

Pacific Daylight Saving Time ends 2:00AM November 4th. Turn clocks back one hour.

Day	☉	☿	♀	♂	♃	♄	♅	♆	♇	Mean Node
1	10♐	20♏	12♏	11♑	11♉R	07♏	05♈R	00♒	08♑	25♏
2	11	21	14	12	11	07	05	00	08	25
3	12	22	15	13	11	07	05	00	08	25
4	13	23	16	14	11	07	05	00	08	25
5	14	24	17	15	11	07	05	00	08	25
6	15	25	19	16	10	08	05	00	08	25
7	16	26	20	17	10	08	05	00	08	25
8	17	27	21	18	10	08	05	01	08	25
9	18	28	22	20	10	08	05	01	09	24
10	19	00♐	24	21	09	08	05	01	09	24
11	20	01	25	22	09	08	05	01	09	24
12	21	03	26	23	09	09	05	01	09	24
13	22	04	27	24	09	09	05D	01	09	24
14	23	05	29	25	09	09	05	01	09	24
15	24	07	00♐	26	09	09	05	01	09	24
16	25	08	01	28	09	09	05	01	09	24
17	26	10	04	00♒	09	09	05	01	09	24
18	27	11	04	01	09	09	05	01	09	24
19	28	13	06	02	08	09	05	01	09	24
20	29	14	07	03	08	09	05	01	09	24
21	00♑	16	09	04	08	10	05	01	09	24
22	01	18	10	05	08	10	05	01	09	24
23	02	19	12	—	08	10	05	01	09	24
24	03	18	13	—	08	10	05	01	09	24
25	04	20	15	—	08	10	05	01	09	24
26	05	23	16	00♒	08	10	05	01	09	24
27	06	25	17	01	08	10	05	01	09	24
28	07	26	18	02	08	10	05	01	09	24
29	08	28	19	03	08	10	05	01	09	24
30	10♑	29	19	04	08	10	05	01	09	24
31	11	01♑	08	05	08	10	05	01	09	24

Above are rounded to nearest whole degree. Positions more than 29°30' round to 30° of one sign before 00° of the next sign. See pages 50–61 for a complete ephemeris.

December Planting Days
Above-ground crops: Best: 18, 19   Good: 14, 15, 22, 23, 24
Root crops/perennials: Best: 1, 2, 10, 11, 28, 29   Good: 7, 8, 9

Planets Visible in the Morning Sky
Mercury, Venus, Jupiter through the 3rd, and Saturn. **Do not confuse** Venus with Saturn early month; Venus is brighter.
Planets Visible in the Evening Sky
Mars, and Jupiter from the 3rd.

SAGITTARIUS ♐
November 21 to December 21 "I PERCEIVE"
A mutable, fire sign of positive polarity.
SYMBOL: the centaur.   COLORS: purple and deep blue.
RULING PLANET: Jupiter.   RULES: the hips and thighs.
KEYWORDS: aspiring, exploring, freedom-loving, foresightful, optimistic,

Sagittarius

DECEMBER 2012

NOVEMBER 2012

S	M	T	W	T	F	S
				1	2	3
4	5	6	7	8	9	10
11	12	13	14	15	16	17
18	19	20	21	22	23	24
25	26	27	28	29	30	

JANUARY 2013

S	M	T	W	T	F	S
		1	2	3	4	5
6	7	8	9	10	11	12
13	14	15	16	17	18	19
20	21	22	23	24	25	26
27	28	29	30	31		

Moon goes void-of-course, Moon enters next sign.
First Qtr 28♓44 9:19p — ☽v/c 9:19p ☽→♈ 11:43p
♀△♅ 1:39p ☽✶♂ 2:44p ☽□☉ 9:19p
Daily aspects (when exact)
Sign or Direction changes

						1 ☽ in ♋ ☽v/c 10:55p ☽☍♂ 4:01a ☽△♀ 5:40a ☽△☿ 10:55p
2 ☽→♌ 5:57p SAGITTARIUS ☉☍♃ 5:45p Advent Sunday	**3** ☽ in ♌ ☽△♅ 3:06a ☽□♄ 7:30a ☽✶♃ 3:50p ☽△☉ 6:04p ☽□♀ 11:38p	**4** ☽ in ♌ ☽v/c 2:08p ☽□☿ 2:08p	**5** ☽→♍ 3:51a ☽☍♆ 4:52a ☽✶♄ 5:14p ☽△♇ 7:35p	**6** ☽ in ♍ Last Qtr 14♍55 7:31a ☽□♃ 0:04a ☽△♂ 7:31a ☽□☉ 7:31a ☽✶♀ 1:54p	**7** ☽v/c 2:35a ☽→♎ 10:35a ☽✶☿ 2:35a ☽☍♅ 6:43p	**8** ☽ in ♎ ☽v/c 4:37p ☽□♇ 1:27a ☽△♃ 5:00a ☽□♂ 3:34p ☽✶☉ 4:37p
9 ☽→♏ 1:51p Hanukkah ☽△♆ 2:50p	**10** ☽ in ♏ ☽☌♄ 2:21a ☽✶♇ 3:55a ☿→♐ 5:40p ☽✶♂ 7:51p	**11** ☽v/c 5:08a ☽→♐ 2:22p ☿□♆ 4:58a ☽☌♀ 5:08a ☽□♆ 3:22p ☽● ☿ 4:21p ☽△♅ 9:40p	**12** ☽ in ♐ ☽☍♃ 6:12a	**13** ☽v/c 0:42a ☽→♑ 1:43p New Moon 21♐45 0:42a ☽☌☉ 0:42a ♅SD 4:02a ☽✶♆ 2:46p ☽□♅ 9:01p Geminids meteors	**14** ☽ in ♑ ☽✶♄ 2:24a ☿△♅ 3:25a ☽● ♇ 3:30a	**15** ☽v/c 1:15p ☽→♒ 1:53p ☽☌♂ 0:17a ☽✶♀ 1:15p ♀→♐ 8:38p ☽✶♅ 9:30p
16 ☽ in ♒ ☽✶☿ 2:03a ☽□♄ 3:27a ☽△♃ 5:38a ♀□♆ 10:25a	**17** ☽v/c 10:11a ☽→♓ 4:48p ☽✶☉ 10:11a ☿☍♃ 11:22a ☽☌♆ 6:07p ☽□♀ 9:17p	**18** ☽ in ♓ ☽△♄ 7:46a ☽✶♇ 8:34a ☽□♃ 9:16a ☽□☿ 12:10p	**19** ☽v/c 9:19p ☽→♈ 11:43p First Qtr 28♓44 9:19p ♀△♅ 1:39p ☽✶♂ 2:44p ☽□☉ 9:19p	**20** ☽ in ♈ ☽☌♅ 8:34a ☽△♀ 10:40a ☽□♇ 4:51p ☽✶♃ 4:54p	**21** ☽ in ♈ ☉→♑ 3:12a ☽△☿ 4:13a ☉✶♆ 10:49p **Winter Solstice** **Sun enters Capricorn**	**22** ☽v/c 4:57a ☽→♉ 10:25a ☽□♂ 4:57a ☽✶♆ 12:07p ☽△☉ 1:19p ♀☍♃ 7:50p
23 ☽ in ♉ ☽☍♄ 4:13a ☽△♇ 4:35a	**24** ☽v/c 9:58p ☽→♊ 11:13p ☽△♂ 9:58p	**25** ☽ in ♊ ☽□♆ 1:04a ☽✶♅ 8:45a ☽● ♃ 4:18p ♂→♒ 4:49p Christmas ☉□♅ 5:32p	**26** ☽ in ♊ ☽v/c 10:50p CAPRICORN ☽☍♀ 1:09a ♄✶♇ 4:48p Kwanzaa ☽☍☿ 10:50p	**27** ☽→♋ 12:06p ☽△♆ 2:04p ☽□♅ 9:34p	**28** ☽ in ♋ ☽v/c 6:43a Full Moon 7♋06 2:21a ☽☍☉ 2:21a ☽☍♇ 6:34a ☽△♄ 6:43a	**29** ☽→♌ 11:45p No exact aspects
30 ☽ in ♌ ☽△♅ 9:01a ☉✶♄ 9:45a ☉☌♇ 5:37a ☽✶♃ 3:07p ☽☍♂ 6:47a ☽□♄ 6:14p	**31** ☽ in ♌ ☽v/c 1:52p ☽△♀ 1:52p ♂✶♅ 6:32p ☿→♑ 6:03a ☿✶♆ 10:51p					

Pacific Standard Time

JANUARY 2013

SUNDAY	MONDAY	TUESDAY	WEDNESDAY	THURSDAY	FRIDAY	SATURDAY
		1 ☽→♍ 9:35a CAPRICORN ☽☍♆ 11:39a ☽△☿ 1:23p ☽□♃ 11:59p New Year's Day	**2** ☽ in ♍ ☽△♇ 3:12a ☽✶♄ 3:45a ☽△☉ 8:59a	**3** ☽v/c 4:15a ☽→♎ 5:11p ☽□♀ 4:15a ☿□♅ 8:29a	Last Qtr 14♎58 7:58p ☽ in ♎ ☽☍♅ 1:52a ☽□☿ 4:08a ♂△♃ 4:46a ☽△♃ 6:35a ☽△♂ 6:43a ☽□♇ 10:10a ☽□☉ 7:58p	**5** ☽v/c 3:13p ☽→♏ 10:09p ☽✶♀ 3:13p
6 ☽ in ♏ ☽△♆ 0:15a ☿☌♇ 8:42a ☽□♂ 2:05p ☽✶♇ 2:24p ☽✶☿ 3:06p ☽☌♄ 3:10p ☿✶♄ 3:44p	**7** ☽ in ♏ ☽v/c 3:31a ☽✶☉ 3:31a ♂□♄ 11:33a	**8** ☽→♐ 0:28a ☽v/c 6:28p ☽□♆ 2:35a ☽△♅ 8:29a ☽☍♃ 12:05p ☽✶♂ 6:28p ♀→♑ 8:11p	**9** ☽v/c in ♐ ♀✶♆ 9:46p	**10** ☽→♑ 0:54a ☽✶♆ 3:04a ☽☌♀ 3:31a ☽□♅ 8:49a ☽☌♇ 4:22p ☽✶♄ 5:18p	New Moon 21♑46 11:44a ☽ in ♑ ☽v/c 11:44a ☽☌☿ 4:25a ☽☌☉ 11:44a	**12** ☽→♒ 1:01a ☽✶♅ 9:09a ☽△♃ 12:11p ☽□♄ 5:58p ♀□♅ 8:13p
13 ☽ in ♒ ☽v/c 0:37a ☽☌♂ 0:37a	**14** ☽→♓ 2:49a ☽☌♆ 5:21a ☽□♃ 2:26p ☽✶♀ 3:21p ☽✶♇ 7:48p ☽△♄ 9:01p	**15** ☽ in ♓ ☽✶☿ 10:54p	**16** ☽v/c 1:32a ☽→♈ 8:07a ☽✶☉ 1:32a ♀☌♇ 5:27p ☽☌♅ 5:38p ☽✶♃ 8:28p	**17** ☽ in ♈ ☽□♇ 2:38a ☽□♀ 3:37a ♀✶♄ 8:03a ☽✶♂ 6:27p	First Qtr 29♈04 3:45p ☽v/c 4:40p ☽→♉ 5:36p ☉☌☿ 0:56a ☽□☉ 3:45p ☽□☿ 4:40p ☽✶♆ 8:49p ☿→♒ 11:25p	**19** ☽ in ♉ ☽△♇ 1:30p ☉→♒ 1:52p ☽☍♄ 3:05p ☽△♀ 9:17p **Sun enters Aquarius**
20 ☽ in ♉ ☽v/c 10:16a ☽□♂ 10:16a	**21** ☽→♊ 6:04a ☽□♆ 9:34a ☽△☉ 9:53a ☽△☿ 3:13p ☽✶♅ 4:49p ☽●♃ 7:13p Martin L. King Jr. Day	**22** ☽ in ♊ AQUARIUS ☿✶♅ 2:28a ☿△♃ 6:26p	**23** ☽v/c 3:42a ☽→♋ 7:00p ☽△♂ 3:42a ☽△♆ 10:37p	**24** ☽ in ♋ ☽□♅ 5:45a ☽☍♇ 3:18p ☽△♄ 5:00p ☉✶♅ 8:45p	**25** ☽ in ♋ ☽v/c 12:35p ☿□♄ 10:42a ☽☍♀ 12:35p ☉△♃ 7:56p	Full Moon 7♌24 8:38p ☽→♌ 6:20a ☽△♅ 4:52p ☽✶♃ 6:36p ☽☍☉ 8:38p
27 ☽ in ♌ ☽□♄ 3:43a ☽☍☿ 10:09a	**28** ☽v/c 8:59a ☽→♍ 3:27p ☽☍♂ 8:59a ☽☍♆ 7:08p	**29** ☽ in ♍ ☽□♃ 3:14a ☽△♇ 10:36a ☽✶♄ 12:13p	**30** ☽v/c 5:59p ☽→♎ 10:36p ♃SD 3:37a ☉□♄ 2:49p ☽△♀ 5:59p	**31** ☽ in ♎ ☽☍♅ 8:43a ☽△♃ 10:00a ☽□♇ 5:16p ☽△☉ 9:04p		DECEMBER 2012

DECEMBER 2012

S	M	T	W	T	F	S
						1
2	3	4	5	6	7	8
9	10	11	12	13	14	15
16	17	18	19	20	21	22
23	24	25	26	27	28	29
30	31					

FEBRUARY 2013

					1 D in ♎ D v/c 5:03p D△☿ 5:03p ♂→♓ 5:54p ♀→♒ 6:47p	**2** D→♏ 4:02a D△♂ 4:39a D□♀ 4:57a D△♆ 7:45a D✶♇ 10:14p Candlemas D☌♄ 11:45p Groundhog Day
3 D in ♏ Last Qtr 14♏54 5:56a D□☉ 5:56a	**4** D v/c 4:31a D→♐ 7:45a D□☿ 4:31a D□♂ 11:25a D□♆ 11:30a ♂☌♆ 12:57p D✶♀ 1:40p D△♅ 5:33p D☍♃ 6:32p	**5** D in ♐ D v/c 12:42p ☿→♓ 6:56a D✶☉ 12:42p	**6** D→♑ 9:55a ♀✶♅ 11:08a D✶☿ 1:31p D✶♆ 1:42p ☿☌♆ 3:00p D✶♂ 4:21p D□♅ 7:37p ♀△♃ 9:58p	**7** D in ♑ D v/c 4:44a D☌♇ 3:20a D✶♄ 4:44a	**8** D→♒ 11:17a ☿☌♂ 9:57a D✶♅ 9:07p D△♃ 9:59p	**9** D in ♒ D v/c 11:20p New Moon 21♒43 11:20p D☌♀ 2:25a ☿□♃ 4:08a D□♄ 6:12a D☌☉ 11:20p
10 D→♓ 1:20p ♂□♃ 0:12a D☌♆ 5:29p Chinese ♀□♄ 10:42p New Year: the Snake	**11** D in ♓ D v/c 9:03a D□♃ 0:33a D☌♂ 1:56a D☌☿ 6:00a D✶♇ 7:40a D△♄ 9:03a ☿✶♇ 9:58p	**12** D→♈ 5:51p Mardi Gras ☿△♄ 11:15a Shrove Tuesday	**13** D in ♈ D☌♅ 5:05a D✶♃ 6:01a D□♇ 1:34p D✶♀ 9:51p Ash Wednesday	**14** D in ♈ D v/c 7:35p D✶☉ 7:35p St. Valentine's Day	**15** D→♉ 2:08a D✶♆ 7:13a ♂✶♇ 10:14a D△♇ 11:20p	**16** D in ♉ D✶♂ 0:13a D☍♄ 0:44a ♂△♄ 8:14a D✶☿ 10:21a D□♀ 2:48p
17 D v/c 12:31p D→♊ 1:50p First Qtr 29♉21 12:31p D□☉ 12:31p D□♆ 7:20p	**18** D in ♊ D✶♅ 2:49a D☌♃ 3:54a ☉→♓ 4:02a ♄SR 9:03a D□♂ 5:02p Presidents Day **Sun enters Pisces**	**19** D in ♊ D v/c 10:48a D□☿ 3:39a D△♀ 10:48a	**20** D→♋ 2:45a D△☉ 7:04a D△♆ 8:24a D□♅ 3:52p ☉☌♆ 11:19p	**21** D in ♋ D v/c 6:08p D☍♇ 0:43a D△♄ 1:52a D△♂ 9:47a D△☿ 6:08p	**22** D→♌ 2:12p No exact aspects	**23** D in ♌ ☿SR 1:41a D△♅ 3:00a D✶♃ 4:14a D□♄ 12:16p
24 D v/c 8:50p D→♍ 10:52p Purim D☍♀ 8:50p	**25** D in ♍ Full Moon 7♍24 12:26p D☍♆ 4:22a D☍☉ 12:26p D□♃ 12:35p ☉□♃ 2:26p ♀→♓ 6:03p D△♇ 7:05p D✶♄ 7:51p	**26** D in ♍ D v/c 10:13a ☿☌♂ 1:09a D☍☿ 9:22a D☍♂ 10:13a	**27** D→♎ 5:02a D☍♅ 5:11p D△♃ 6:35p	**28** D in ♎ D v/c 0:37a D□♇ 0:37a ♀☌♆ 5:37a		**MARCH 2013** S M T W T F S 1 2 3 4 5 6 7 8 9 10 11 12 13 14 15 16 17 18 19 20 21 22 23 24 25 26 27 28 29 30 31

Pacific Standard Time

JANUARY 2012 — Noon Greenwich Mean Time

Day	☉	☽	☿	♀	♂	♃	♄	♅	♆	♇
	° ′ ″	° ′ ″	° ′	° ′	° ′	° ′	° ′	° ′	° ′	° ′
🌓 1	10♑28 00	13♈04 25	20♐30	14♒26	20♍14	0♉26	28♎19	0♈51	28♒54	7♑20
2	11 29 09	24 56 00	21 52	15 40	20 28	0 28	28 23	0 52	28 56	7 22
3	12 30 18	6♉45 32	23 14	16 53	20 41	0 30	28 27	0 54	28 58	7 25
4	13 31 27	18 37 53	24 38	18 07	20 54	0 31	28 30	0 55	28 59	7 27
5	14 32 36	0♊37 33	26 02	19 20	21 07	0 34	28 33	0 56	29 01	7 29
6	15 33 44	12 48 21	27 27	20 34	21 19	0 36	28 37	0 57	29 03	7 31
7	16 34 52	25 13 18	28 53	21 47	21 30	0 38	28 40	0 59	29 05	7 33
8	17 36 00	7♋54 20	0♑20	23 00	21 41	0 41	28 43	1 00	29 06	7 35
🌕 9	18 37 07	20 52 12	1 47	24 13	21 51	0 44	28 46	1 02	29 08	7 37
10	19 38 15	4♌06 28	3 15	25 27	22 00	0 47	28 49	1 03	29 10	7 40
11	20 39 22	17 35 37	4 43	26 40	22 09	0 50	28 52	1 05	29 12	7 42
12	21 40 29	1♍17 21	6 12	27 53	22 18	0 54	28 55	1 07	29 14	7 44
13	22 41 36	15 08 59	7 42	29 06	22 25	0 57	28 57	1 08	29 16	7 46
14	23 42 43	29 07 50	9 12	0♓19	22 33	1 01	29 00	1 10	29 18	7 48
15	24 43 49	13♎11 34	10 43	1 32	22 39	1 05	29 02	1 12	29 20	7 50
🌗 16	25 44 56	27 18 20	12 14	2 45	22 45	1 10	29 05	1 14	29 21	7 52
17	26 46 02	11♏26 38	13 46	3 57	22 50	1 14	29 07	1 15	29 23	7 54
18	27 47 08	25 35 08	15 18	5 10	22 54	1 19	29 09	1 17	29 25	7 56
19	28 48 14	9♐42 16	16 51	6 23	22 58	1 23	29 11	1 19	29 27	7 58
20	29 49 20	23 45 58	18 25	7 35	23 01	1 28	29 13	1 21	29 29	8 00
21	0♒50 25	7♑43 34	19 59	8 48	23 03	1 34	29 15	1 23	29 32	8 02
22	1 51 30	21 31 52	21 33	10 00	23 05	1 39	29 17	1 25	29 34	8 04
🌑 23	2 52 34	5♒07 34	23 08	11 13	23 05	1 45	29 18	1 27	29 36	8 06
24	3 53 38	18 27 42	24 44	12 25	23R05	1 50	29 20	1 30	29 38	8 08
25	4 54 40	1♓30 16	26 20	13 37	23 05	1 56	29 21	1 32	29 40	8 10
26	5 55 41	14 14 29	27 57	14 49	23 03	2 02	29 23	1 34	29 42	8 12
27	6 56 42	26 41 06	29 35	16 01	23 01	2 08	29 24	1 36	29 44	8 14
28	7 57 41	8♈52 16	1♒13	17 13	22 58	2 15	29 25	1 39	29 46	8 16
29	8 58 40	20 51 24	2 52	18 25	22 54	2 21	29 26	1 41	29 48	8 18
30	9 59 37	2♉42 52	4 31	19 37	22 50	2 28	29 27	1 43	29 51	8 20
🌓 31	11 00 33	14 31 44	6 11	20 48	22 44	2 35	29 28	1 46	29 53	8 22

Day	Sidereal Time	True ☊	DECLINATIONS ☉	☽	☿	♀	♂	♃	♄	♅	♆	♇
	H M S	° ′	° ′	° ′	° ′	° ′	° ′	° ′	° ′	° ′	° ′	° ′
1	18:42:14	13D58	23S01	9N23	22S15	18S15	6N35	10N29	8S37	0S19	12S22	19S19
3	18:50:07	14♐01	22 51	16 46	22 41	17 30	6 27	10 30	8 39	0 18	12 21	19 19
5	18:58:00	14 04	22 39	21 28	23 04	16 43	6 20	10 32	8 41	0 17	12 20	19 19
7	19:05:53	14R04	22 24	22 20	23 23	15 54	6 14	10 34	8 43	0 16	12 18	19 19
9	19:13:46	13 58	22 09	18 44	23 38	15 04	6 09	10 37	8 44	0 15	12 17	19 19
11	19:21:39	13 47	21 51	11 08	23 48	14 12	6 05	10 40	8 46	0 14	12 16	19 19
13	19:29:32	13 35	21 32	1 05	23 53	13 19	6 02	10 43	8 47	0 12	12 14	19 19
15	19:37:25	13 28	21 11	9S21	23 53	12 24	6 00	10 46	8 49	0 11	12 13	19 19
17	19:45:19	13D28	20 48	17 52	23 48	11 28	5 59	10 50	8 50	0 09	12 12	19 19
19	19:53:12	13 30	20 24	22 15	23 38	10 31	5 59	10 53	8 51	0 08	12 10	19 19
21	20:01:05	13R27	19 58	21 06	23 23	9 33	6 00	10 58	8 52	0 06	12 09	19 18
23	20:08:58	13 15	19 31	15 04	23 02	8 34	6 02	11 02	8 52	0 04	12 07	19 18
25	20:16:51	12 56	19 02	6 16	22 35	7 34	6 06	11 06	8 53	0 02	12 06	19 18
27	20:24:44	12 38	18 32	3N14	22 03	6 34	6 10	11 11	8 53	0 01	12 04	19 18
29	20:32:37	12 28	18 01	11 51	21 24	5 32	6 16	11 16	8 54	0N01	12 03	19 18
31	20:40:30	12D25	17 28	18 29	20 40	4 31	6 23	11 21	8 54	0 03	12 01	19 18

Eris ⯰ Jan. 1, 2012 21°♈23′28″℞ SD=Jan. 10 21°♈23′07″

Day	☉	☽	☿	♀	♂	♃	♄	♅	♆	♇
1	12≈01 27	26♉23 22	7≈52	22♓00	22♍38	2♉42	29♎29	1♈48	29≈55	8♑24
2	13 02 21	8♊23 11	9 33	23 11	22♍31	2 49	29 29	1 51	29 57	8 25
3	14 03 13	20 36 15	11 16	24 23	22 23	2 57	29 30	1 53	29 59	8 27
4	15 04 04	3♋06 58	12 59	25 34	22 15	3 04	29 30	1 56	0♓02	8 29
5	16 04 53	15 58 32	14 42	26 45	22 05	3 12	29 30	1 58	0 04	8 31
6	17 05 41	29 12 32	16 27	27 56	21 55	3 20	29 30	2 01	0 06	8 33
☽ 7	18 06 28	12♌48 34	18 12	29 07	21 44	3 28	29 30	2 04	0 08	8 34
8	19 07 14	26 44 08	19 58	0♈18	21 33	3 36	29R30	2 06	0 10	8 36
9	20 07 58	10♍54 50	21 44	1 28	21 20	3 44	29 30	2 09	0 13	8 38
10	21 08 41	25 14 52	23 32	2 39	21 07	3 52	29 30	2 12	0 15	8 40
11	22 09 23	9♎38 49	25 20	3 49	20 53	4 01	29 30	2 15	0 17	8 41
12	23 10 04	24 00 54	27 08	4 59	20 39	4 09	29 29	2 17	0 20	8 43
13	24 10 44	8♏11 03	28 58	6 09	20 23	4 18	29 29	2 20	0 22	8 44
☽14	25 11 23	22 25 43	0♓47	7 19	20 07	4 27	29 28	2 23	0 24	8 46
15	26 12 01	6♐25 01	2 38	8 29	19 50	4 36	29 27	2 26	0 26	8 47
16	27 12 37	20 15 04	4 28	9 39	19 33	4 46	29 26	2 29	0 29	8 49
17	28 13 13	3♑56 02	6 19	10 48	19 15	4 55	29 24	2 32	0 31	8 51
18	29 13 47	17 27 53	8 10	11 58	18 56	5 04	29 24	2 35	0 33	8 53
19	0♓14 20	0≈50 10	10 00	13 07	18 37	5 14	29 23	2 38	0 35	8 54
20	1 14 51	14 01 54	11 51	14 16	18 17	5 24	29 22	2 41	0 38	8 55
☽21	2 15 21	27 01 50	13 41	15 25	17 56	5 34	29 20	2 44	0 40	8 57
22	3 15 50	9♓48 46	15 29	16 34	17 36	5 44	29 19	2 47	0 42	8 58
23	4 16 16	22 21 58	17 17	17 43	17 14	5 54	29 17	2 50	0 45	9 00
24	5 16 41	4♈41 30	19 03	18 51	16 52	6 04	29 16	2 53	0 47	9 01
25	6 17 04	16 48 38	20 47	19 59	16 30	6 14	29 14	2 56	0 49	9 02
26	7 17 26	28 45 31	22 29	21 07	16 08	6 25	29 12	3 00	0 52	9 04
27	8 17 45	10♉35 35	24 08	22 15	15 45	6 35	29 10	3 03	0 54	9 05
28	9 18 03	22 23 06	25 43	23 23	15 22	6 46	29 08	3 06	0 56	9 06
29	10 18 18	4♊13 05	27 14	24 30	14 58	6 56	29 06	3 09	0 58	9 08

Day	Sidereal Time	True ☊					DECLINATIONS					
			☉	☽	☿	♀	♂	♃	♄	♅	♆	♇
	H M S		° '	° '	° '	° '	° '	° '	° '	° '	° '	° '
1	20:44:27	12D26	17S11	20N43	20S16	4S00	6N27	11N24	8S54	0N04	12S01	19S18
3	20:52:20	12R27	16 37	22 23	19 23	2 57	6 36	11 29	8 53	0 06	11 59	19 17
5	21:00:13	12↗20	16 01	19 41	18 25	1 55	6 45	11 35	8 53	0 08	11 58	19 17
7	21:08:06	12 09	15 24	12 44	17 20	0 52	6 56	11 41	8 53	0 11	11 56	19 17
9	21:15:59	11 41	14 46	2 48	16 10	0N11	7 08	11 47	8 52	0 13	11 54	19 17
11	21:23:52	11 22	14 07	7S54	14 53	1 14	7 21	11 53	8 52	0 15	11 53	19 17
13	21:31:46	11 13	13 28	16 52	13 32	2 17	7 35	11 59	8 51	0 17	11 51	19 16
15	21:39:39	11D12	12 47	21 48	12 04	3 19	7 50	12 06	8 50	0 20	11 50	19 16
17	21:47:32	11R10	12 05	21 25	10 32	4 22	8 05	12 13	8 49	0 22	11 48	19 16
19	21:55:25	10 59	11 23	16 13	8 56	5 24	8 21	12 19	8 47	0 24	11 46	19 16
21	22:03:18	10 36	10 40	7 55	7 16	6 25	8 38	12 26	8 46	0 27	11 45	19 16
23	22:11:11	10 08	9 57	1N28	5 34	7 26	8 55	12 33	8 44	0 29	11 43	19 16
25	22:19:04	9 45	9 12	10 18	3 51	8 26	9 13	12 40	8 43	0 31	11 41	19 15
27	22:26:57	9 32	8 27	17 19	2 09	9 26	9 30	12 48	8 41	0 34	11 40	19 15
29	22:34:50	9 29	7 42	21 27	0 31	10 25	9 48	12 55	8 39	0 37	11 38	19 15

Eris ♓ Feb. 1, 2012 21°♈26'03"

51

Day	☉	☽	☿	♀	♂	♃	♄	♅	♆	♇
❍ 1	11♓18 32	16Ⅱ11 00	28♓40	25♈38	14R35	7♉07	29R03	3♈12	1♓01	9♑09
2	12 18 43	28 22 28	0♈01	26 45	14♏11	7 18	29♎01	3 16	1 03	9 10
3	13 18 53	10♋52 46	1 16	27 51	13 48	7 29	28 59	3 19	1 05	9 11
4	14 19 00	23 46 24	2 25	28 58	13 24	7 40	28 56	3 22	1 07	9 12
5	15 19 05	7♌06 21	3 26	0♉04	13 00	7 52	28 53	3 25	1 09	9 13
6	16 19 09	20 53 27	4 21	1 10	12 36	8 03	28 51	3 29	1 12	9 14
7	17 19 10	5♍05 47	5 07	2 16	12 13	8 14	28 48	3 32	1 14	9 16
☽ 8	18 19 09	19 38 33	5 45	3 22	11 49	8 26	28 45	3 35	1 16	9 17
9	19 19 06	4♎24 34	6 14	4 27	11 26	8 38	28 42	3 39	1 18	9 18
10	20 19 02	19 15 19	6 35	5 32	11 03	8 49	28 39	3 42	1 20	9 19
11	21 18 55	4♏02 33	6 46	6 37	10 40	9 01	28 36	3 46	1 23	9 19
12	22 18 48	18 39 26	6R49	7 42	10 18	9 13	28 33	3 49	1 25	9 20
13	23 18 38	3♐01 28	6 43	8 46	9 56	9 25	28 31	3 52	1 27	9 21
14	24 18 27	17 06 27	6 29	9 50	9 34	9 37	28 26	3 56	1 29	9 22
❍ 15	25 18 14	0♑54 06	6 07	10 54	9 12	9 49	28 23	3 59	1 31	9 23
16	26 18 00	14 25 22	5 38	11 57	8 52	10 01	28 19	4 02	1 33	9 24
17	27 17 44	27 41 45	5 02	13 00	8 31	10 13	28 16	4 06	1 35	9 24
18	28 17 26	10♒44 44	4 20	14 03	8 11	10 26	28 12	4 09	1 38	9 25
19	29 17 06	23 35 34	3 34	15 05	7 52	10 38	28 08	4 13	1 40	9 26
20	0♈16 44	6♓15 03	2 44	16 07	7 33	10 51	28 05	4 16	1 42	9 27
21	1 16 21	18 43 43	1 51	17 09	7 15	11 03	28 01	4 20	1 44	9 27
❍ 22	2 15 55	1♈01 58	0 57	18 10	6 58	11 16	27 57	4 23	1 46	9 28
23	3 15 28	13 10 24	0 03	19 11	6 41	11 28	27 53	4 26	1 48	9 28
24	4 14 58	25 10 03	29♓19	20 12	6 25	11 41	27 49	4 30	1 50	9 29
25	5 14 26	7♉02 37	28 19	21 12	6 09	11 54	27 45	4 33	1 52	9 30
26	6 13 53	18 50 33	27 30	22 11	5 54	12 07	27 41	4 37	1 54	9 30
27	7 13 17	0Ⅱ37 10	26 44	23 10	5 40	12 20	27 37	4 40	1 56	9 31
28	8 12 38	12 26 32	26 05	24 10	5 27	12 33	27 33	4 44	1 58	9 31
29	9 11 58	24 23 21	25 30	25 08	5 15	12 46	27 28	4 47	2 00	9 31
❍ 30	10 11 15	6♋32 48	24 59	26 06	5 03	12 59	27 24	4 50	2 02	9 32
31	11 10 30	19 00 09	24 34	27 03	4 52	13 12	27 20	4 54	2 04	9 32

Day	Sidereal Time	True ☊					DECLINATIONS					
			☉	☽	☿	♀	♂	♃	♄	♅	♆	♇
1	22:38:47	9R29	7S19	22N08	0N16	10N54	9N57	12N59	8S38	0N38	11S38	19S15
3	22:46:40	9♑26	6 33	20 22	1 44	11 51	10 14	13 06	8 36	0 41	11 36	19 15
5	22:54:33	9 14	5 47	14 22	3 02	12 47	10 31	13 14	8 34	0 44	11 35	19 15
7	23:02:26	8 53	5 01	4 59	4 06	13 43	10 47	13 22	8 31	0 46	11 33	19 14
9	23:10:19	8 30	4 14	5S54	4 56	14 37	11 03	13 29	8 29	0 49	11 31	19 14
11	23:18:13	8 14	3 27	15 32	5 29	15 29	11 18	13 37	8 26	0 52	11 30	19 14
13	23:26:06	8 10	2 39	21 12	5 43	16 21	11 32	13 45	8 24	0 54	11 28	19 14
15	23:33:59	8R10	1 52	21 28	5 39	17 10	11 45	13 53	8 21	0 57	11 27	19 14
17	23:41:52	8 05	1 05	16 51	5 16	17 59	11 57	14 01	8 18	1 00	11 25	19 14
19	23:49:45	7 59	0 17	9 02	4 38	18 46	12 09	14 09	8 15	1 02	11 24	19 13
21	23:57:38	7 38	0N30	0N05	3 47	19 31	12 18	14 17	8 12	1 05	11 23	19 13
23	0:05:31	7 14	1 18	8 58	2 47	20 14	12 27	14 25	8 09	1 08	11 21	19 13
25	0:13:24	6 53	2 05	16 15	1 44	20 56	12 35	14 33	8 06	1 11	11 20	19 13
27	0:21:17	6 42	2 52	20 48	0 41	21 36	12 41	14 42	8 03	1 13	11 18	19 13
29	0:29:10	6D41	3 39	21 45	0S17	22 14	12 46	14 50	8 00	1 16	11 17	19 13
31	0:37:04	6R41	4 25	18 40	1 08	22 50	12 50	14 58	7 57	1 19	11 16	19 13

Eris ♓ March 1, 2012   21°♈37'17"

APRIL 2012 — Noon Greenwich Mean Time

Day	☉ ° ′ ″	☽ ° ′ ″	☿ ° ′	♀ ° ′	♂ ° ′	♃ ° ′	♄ ° ′	♅ ° ′	♆ ° ′	♇ ° ′
1	12♈09 43	1♌50 21	24R15	28♉00	4R42	13♉25	27R15	4♈57	2♓05	9♑32
2	13 08 53	15 07 20	24♓01	28 57	4♍33	13 39	27♎11	5 01	2 07	9 33
3	14 08 01	28 53 20	23 53	29 52	4 24	13 52	27 07	5 04	2 09	9 33
4	15 07 06	13♍08 00	23D51	0♊48	4 16	14 05	27 02	5 07	2 11	9 33
5	16 06 09	27 47 54	23 54	1 42	4 09	14 19	26 58	5 11	2 12	9 33
○ 6	17 05 11	12♎46 24	24 03	2 36	4 03	14 32	26 53	5 14	2 14	9 33
7	18 04 10	27 54 33	24 16	3 30	3 58	14 46	26 49	5 18	2 16	9 33
8	19 03 07	13♏02 21	24 35	4 22	3 53	14 59	26 44	5 21	2 18	9 34
9	20 02 03	28 00 34	24 58	5 14	3 49	15 13	26 40	5 24	2 19	9 34
10	21 00 56	12♐41 58	25 26	6 06	3 46	15 26	26 35	5 28	2 21	9 34
11	21 59 48	27 02 05	25 58	6 56	3 44	15 40	26 30	5 31	2 23	9R34
12	22 58 38	10♑59 06	26 34	7 46	3 42	15 54	26 26	5 34	2 24	9 34
◑ 13	23 57 27	24 33 18	27 14	8 35	3 41	16 07	26 21	5 38	2 26	9 33
14	24 56 14	7♒46 23	27 58	9 24	3D41	16 21	26 17	5 41	2 27	9 33
15	25 54 59	20 40 51	28 46	10 11	3 42	16 35	26 12	5 44	2 29	9 33
16	26 53 42	3♓19 22	29 36	10 58	3 43	16 49	26 07	5 47	2 30	9 33
17	27 52 24	15 44 31	0♈30	11 44	3 45	17 03	26 03	5 51	2 32	9 33
18	28 51 03	27 58 38	1 27	12 29	3 48	17 17	25 58	5 54	2 33	9 33
19	29 49 41	10♈03 42	2 27	13 12	3 51	17 31	25 54	5 57	2 35	9 32
20	0♉48 17	22 01 32	3 30	13 55	3 55	17 45	25 49	6 00	2 36	9 32
● 21	1 46 52	3♉53 52	4 35	14 37	4 00	17 58	25 44	6 03	2 38	9 32
22	2 45 24	15 42 30	5 43	15 18	4 06	18 12	25 40	6 07	2 39	9 31
23	3 43 55	27 29 35	6 53	15 57	4 12	18 27	25 35	6 10	2 40	9 31
24	4 42 23	9♊17 37	8 06	16 36	4 19	18 41	25 31	6 13	2 42	9 31
25	5 40 50	21 09 39	9 21	17 13	4 26	18 55	25 26	6 16	2 43	9 30
26	6 39 14	3♋09 14	10 38	17 49	4 34	19 09	25 22	6 19	2 44	9 30
27	7 37 37	15 20 25	11 58	18 24	4 43	19 23	25 17	6 22	2 45	9 29
28	8 35 57	27 47 32	13 20	18 57	4 53	19 37	25 13	6 25	2 47	9 29
◐ 29	9 34 15	10♌34 55	14 43	19 29	5 02	19 51	25 08	6 28	2 48	9 28
30	10 32 31	23 46 24	16 09	20 00	5 13	20 05	25 04	6 31	2 49	9 28

Day	Sidereal Time H M S	True ☊ ° ′	DECLINATIONS ☉ ° ′	☽ ° ′	☿ ° ′	♀ ° ′	♂ ° ′	♃ ° ′	♄ ° ′	♅ ° ′	♆ ° ′	♇ ° ′
1	0:41:00	6R39	4N48	15N39	1S30	23N07	12N51	15N02	7S55	1N20	11S15	19S13
3	0:48:53	6♐29	5 34	7 06	2 07	23 40	12 53	15 10	7 52	1 23	11 14	19 13
5	0:56:46	6 14	6 20	3S30	2 34	24 11	12 53	15 18	7 48	1 25	11 13	19 13
7	1:04:39	6 00	7 05	13 41	2 50	24 40	12 53	15 27	7 45	1 28	11 11	19 12
9	1:12:33	5 54	7 50	20 24	2 57	25 07	12 51	15 35	7 42	1 31	11 10	19 12
11	1:20:26	5D55	8 34	21 32	2 53	25 32	12 48	15 43	7 38	1 33	11 09	19 12
13	1:28:19	5R57	9 18	17 23	2 41	25 55	12 45	15 51	7 35	1 36	11 08	19 12
15	1:36:12	5 53	10 01	9 51	2 21	26 16	12 40	15 59	7 32	1 39	11 07	19 12
17	1:44:05	5 43	10 43	0 55	1 52	26 34	12 34	16 07	7 29	1 41	11 06	19 12
19	1:51:58	5 30	11 25	7N55	1 17	26 51	12 27	16 15	7 25	1 44	11 05	19 12
21	1:59:51	5 19	12 06	15 22	0 35	27 05	12 19	16 23	7 22	1 46	11 04	19 12
23	2:07:44	5 14	12 46	20 17	0N14	27 18	12 10	16 31	7 19	1 49	11 03	19 12
25	2:15:37	5D15	13 25	21 42	1 08	27 28	12 01	16 39	7 16	1 51	11 02	19 12
27	2:23:31	5 18	14 03	19 12	2 07	27 36	11 50	16 47	7 12	1 54	11 01	19 12
29	2:31:24	5R20	14 41	12 59	3 11	27 42	11 39	16 55	7 09	1 56	11 00	19 12

Eris ⯰ April 1, 2012 21°♈55′38″

MAY 2012 — Noon Greenwich Mean Time

Day	☉	☽	☿	♀	♂	♃	♄	♅	♆	♇
1	11♉30'46"	7♍24'47"	17♈37	20♊28	5♍24	20♉19	25♎00R	6♈34	2♓50	9♑27R
2	12 28 58	21 31 02	19 06	20 56	5 36	20 34	24♎55△	6 37	2 51	9♑26R
3	13 27 08	6△03 35	20 38	21 21	5 48	20 48	24 51	6 40	2 52	9 26
4	14 25 16	20 57 56	22 12	21 45	6 01	21 02	24 47	6 43	2 53	9 24
5	15 23 22	6♏06 49	23 47	22 08	6 14	21 16	24 43	6 46	2 54	9 24
☽ 6	16 21 27	21 20 54	25 25	22 28	6 28	21 30	24 39	6 48	2 55	9 24
7	17 19 30	6✶30 19	27 04	22 46	6 42	21 45	24 35	6 51	2 56	9 23
8	18 17 31	21 26 01	28 46	23 03	6 57	21 59	24 31	6 54	2 57	9 22
9	19 15 31	6♑01 09	0♊29	23 17	7 12	22 13	24 27	6 57	2 58	9 21
10	20 13 30	20 11 29	2 15	23 30	7 28	22 27	24 23	6 59	2 59	9 20
11	21 11 27	3♒55 31	4 02	23 40	7 44	22 41	24 19	7 02	2 59	9 19
☽ 12	22 09 23	17 13 58	5 51	23 48	8 00	22 56	24 15	7 05	3 00	9 19
13	23 07 18	0♓09 06	7 42	23 54	8 18	23 10	24 11	7 07	3 01	9 18
14	24 05 12	12 44 12	9 35	23 58	8 35	23 24	24 08	7 10	3 02	9 17
15	25 03 04	25 02 55	11 30	24 00	8 53	23 38	24 04	7 13	3 02	9 16
16	26 00 55	7♈08 59	13 27	23R59	9 11	23 53	24 00	7 15	3 03	9 15
17	26 58 45	19 05 54	15 26	23 55	9 30	24 07	23 57	7 18	3 04	9 14
18	27 56 33	0♉56 43	17 27	23 50	9 49	24 21	23 54	7 20	3 04	9 13
19	28 54 21	12 44 47	19 29	23 41	10 09	24 35	23 50	7 23	3 05	9 12
☀ 20	29 52 07	24 32 09	21 33	23 31	10 29	24 49	23 47	7 25	3 05	9 11
21	0♊49 51	6♊21 17	23 39	23 18	10 49	25 04	23 44	7 27	3 06	9 10
22	1 47 35	18 14 27	25 46	23 03	11 10	25 18	23 41	7 30	3 06	9 08
23	2 45 17	0♋13 53	27 55	22 45	11 31	25 32	23 38	7 32	3 07	9 07
24	3 42 57	12 22 00	0♋04	22 25	11 53	25 46	23 34	7 34	3 07	9 06
25	4 40 37	24 41 24	2 15	22 03	12 14	26 00	23 32	7 36	3 07	9 05
26	5 38 14	7♌14 53	4 26	21 38	12 37	26 14	23 29	7 39	3 08	9 04
27	6 35 51	20 05 20	6 38	21 12	12 59	26 28	23 26	7 41	3 08	9 01
☽ 28	7 33 25	3♍15 30	8 50	20 43	13 22	26 42	23 23	7 43	3 08	9 01
29	8 30 59	16 47 37	11 02	20 13	13 45	26 56	23 21	7 45	3 08	9 00
30	9 28 31	0♎42 58	13 13	19 41	14 09	27 10	23 18	7 47	3 09	8 59
31	10 26 01	15 01 15	15 24	19 08	14 32	27 25	23 16	7 49	3 09	8 58

Day	Sidereal Time	True Ω	☉	☽	☿	♀	♂	♃	♄	♅	♆	♇
					DECLINATIONS							
1	2:39:17	5♍R17	15N17	3N55	4N20	27N47	11N27	17N02	7S06	1N58	11S00	19S13
3	2:47:10	5✶12	15 53	6S33	5 33	27 49	11 14	17 10	7 03	2 00	10 59	19 13
5	2:55:03	5 07	16 27	15 58	6 49	27 49	11 00	17 18	7 01	2 03	10 58	19 13
7	3:02:56	5D05	17 00	21 16	8 09	27 48	10 46	17 25	6 58	2 05	10 58	19 13
9	3:10:49	5 07	17 32	20 35	9 32	27 44	10 31	17 33	6 55	2 07	10 57	19 13
11	3:18:42	5 09	18 03	14 52	10 57	27 38	10 15	17 40	6 53	2 09	10 57	19 13
13	3:26:35	5R09	18 33	6 29	12 23	27 30	9 59	17 47	6 50	2 11	10 56	19 13
15	3:34:29	5 08	19 02	2N36	13 51	27 19	9 42	17 55	6 48	2 13	10 56	19 13
17	3:42:22	5 05	19 29	11 00	15 19	27 07	9 25	18 02	6 45	2 15	10 55	19 14
19	3:50:15	5 03	19 55	17 35	16 45	26 52	9 07	18 09	6 43	2 17	10 55	19 14
21	3:58:08	5D03	20 19	21 15	18 10	26 34	8 48	18 16	6 41	2 19	10 54	19 14
23	4:06:01	5 03	20 42	21 14	19 31	26 13	8 29	18 23	6 39	2 21	10 54	19 14
25	4:13:54	5 04	21 04	17 12	20 46	25 51	8 09	18 29	6 37	2 22	10 54	19 14
27	4:21:47	5R03	21 24	9 55	21 55	25 25	7 49	18 36	6 36	2 24	10 54	19 14
29	4:29:40	5D03	21 43	0 22	22 56	24 56	7 28	18 43	6 34	2 25	10 54	19 15
31	4:37:33	5 04	22 01	9S40	23 46	24 25	7 07	18 49	6 33	2 27	10 54	19 15

Eris ♓ May 1, 2012 22°♈15'08"

JUNE 2012 — Noon Greenwich Mean Time

Day	☉	☽	☿	♀	♂	♃	♄	♅	♆	♇
	° ′ ″	° ′ ″	° ′	° ′	° ′	° ′	° ′	° ′	° ′	° ′
1	11♊23 30	29♎40 09	17♊34	18R33	14♍56	27♉39	23R14	7♈51	3♓09	8R56
2	12 20 58	14♏34 59	19 43	17♊57	15 21	27 52	23♎11	7 53	3 09	8♑55
3	13 18 25	29 38 56	21 51	17 20	15 46	28 06	23 09	7 55	3 09	8 54
🌕 4	14 15 51	14♐43 37	23 57	16 43	16 11	28 20	23 07	7 56	3 09	8 52
5	15 13 16	29 40 15	26 01	16 05	16 36	28 34	23 05	7 58	3R09	8 51
6	16 10 41	14♑20 49	28 03	15 28	17 01	28 48	23 03	8 00	3 09	8 50
7	17 08 04	28 39 12	0♋04	14 50	17 27	29 02	23 01	8 02	3 09	8 48
8	18 05 27	12♒31 48	2 02	14 13	17 53	29 16	23 00	8 03	3 09	8 47
9	19 02 49	25 57 31	3 58	13 36	18 19	29 29	22 58	8 05	3 09	8 45
10	20 00 10	8♓57 32	5 51	13 00	18 46	29 43	22 57	8 07	3 09	8 44
🌗 11	20 57 31	21 34 41	7 42	12 26	19 13	29 57	22 55	8 08	3 08	8 43
12	21 54 52	3♈52 54	9 31	11 52	19 40	0♊11	22 54	8 10	3 08	8 41
13	22 52 12	15 56 37	11 17	11 20	20 07	0 24	22 53	8 11	3 08	8 40
14	23 49 32	27 50 28	13 01	10 50	20 35	0 38	22 52	8 12	3 08	8 38
15	24 46 51	9♉38 50	14 43	10 21	21 03	0 51	22 51	8 14	3 07	8 37
16	25 44 10	21 25 47	16 22	9 54	21 31	1 05	22 50	8 15	3 07	8 35
17	26 41 28	3♊14 51	17 58	9 30	21 59	1 18	22 49	8 16	3 06	8 34
18	27 38 46	15 09 04	19 32	9 07	22 27	1 32	22 48	8 18	3 06	8 32
🌑 19	28 36 04	27 10 52	21 03	8 47	22 56	1 45	22 48	8 19	3 06	8 31
20	29 33 21	9♋22 11	22 32	8 29	23 25	1 59	22 47	8 20	3 05	8 29
21	0♋30 38	21 44 32	23 58	8 13	23 54	2 12	22 47	8 21	3 05	8 28
22	1 27 54	4♌19 07	25 22	8 00	24 23	2 25	22 46	8 22	3 04	8 26
23	2 25 09	17 06 57	26 42	7 49	24 53	2 38	22 46	8 23	3 04	8 25
24	3 22 24	0♍09 00	28 01	7 41	25 23	2 52	22 46	8 24	3 03	8 23
25	4 19 38	13 26 08	29 16	7 35	25 53	3 05	22D46	8 25	3 02	8 22
26	5 16 52	26 59 12	0♌29	7 31	26 23	3 18	22 46	8 26	3 02	8 20
🌓 27	6 14 05	10♎48 41	1 38	7 29	26 53	3 31	22 46	8 26	3 01	8 19
28	7 11 18	24 54 34	2 45	7D30	27 24	3 44	22 46	8 27	3 00	8 17
29	8 08 30	9♏15 48	3 49	7 33	27 55	3 56	22 47	8 28	2 59	8 16
30	9 05 42	23 49 59	4 50	7 39	28 25	4 09	22 47	8 28	2 59	8 14

Day	Sidereal Time	True ☊	DECLINATIONS ☉	☽	☿	♀	♂	♃	♄	♅	♆	♇
	H M S	° ′	° ′	° ′	° ′	° ′	° ′	° ′	° ′	° ′	° ′	° ′
1	4:41:30	5♐05	22N09	14S14	24N08	24N09	6N56	18N52	6S32	2N28	10S54	19S15
3	4:49:23	5 05	22 24	20 34	24 43	23 35	6 34	18 59	6 31	2 29	10 54	19 15
5	4:57:16	5R05	22 37	21 14	25 06	23 00	6 12	19 05	6 30	2 31	10 54	19 16
7	5:05:09	5 02	22 49	16 15	25 19	22 23	5 49	19 11	6 29	2 32	10 54	19 16
9	5:13:02	5 00	22 59	7 57	25 22	21 47	5 26	19 17	6 28	2 33	10 54	19 16
11	5:20:56	4D58	23 08	1N19	25 15	21 11	5 03	19 23	6 28	2 34	10 54	19 17
13	5:28:49	5 00	23 15	9 57	25 00	20 36	4 39	19 29	6 27	2 36	10 54	19 17
15	5:36:42	5 03	23 20	16 51	24 37	20 03	4 14	19 34	6 27	2 37	10 55	19 17
17	5:44:35	5 04	23 24	20 58	24 07	19 33	3 50	19 40	6 27	2 37	10 55	19 17
19	5:52:28	5R03	23 26	21 26	23 32	19 05	3 25	19 45	6 27	2 38	10 55	19 18
21	6:00:21	4 56	23 26	17 55	22 52	18 41	2 59	19 51	6 27	2 39	10 56	19 18
23	6:08:14	4 48	23 25	10 57	22 08	18 20	2 34	19 56	6 27	2 40	10 56	19 19
25	6:16:07	4 42	23 22	1 44	21 22	18 02	2 08	20 01	6 28	2 41	10 57	19 19
27	6:24:00	4D40	23 17	8S10	20 33	17 48	1 41	20 06	6 28	2 41	10 57	19 19
29	6:31:54	4 42	23 11	16 42	19 43	17 37	1 15	20 11	6 29	2 42	10 58	19 20

Eris ⯰ June 1, 2012 22°♈32′12″

JULY 2012 — Noon Greenwich Mean Time

Day	☉	☽	☿	♀	♂	♃	♄	♅	♆	♇
	° ′ ″	° ′ ″	° ′	° ′	° ′	° ′	° ′	° ′	° ′	° ′
1	10♋02 53	8♐33 04	5♌47	7♊46	28♍57	4♊22	22♎48	8♈29	2R58	8R13
2	11 00 04	23 19 23	6 41	7 56	29 28	4 35	22 48	8 30	2♓57	8♑11
○ 3	11 57 15	8♑02 09	7 32	8 08	29 59	4 47	22 49	8 30	2 56	8 10
4	12 54 26	22 34 10	8 20	8 21	0♎31	5 00	22 50	8 30	2 55	8 08
5	13 51 37	6♒48 58	9 03	8 37	1 03	5 13	22 51	8 31	2 54	8 07
6	14 48 48	20 41 42	9 43	8 55	1 35	5 25	22 52	8 31	2 53	8 05
7	15 45 59	4♓09 42	10 19	9 14	2 07	5 37	22 53	8 32	2 52	8 04
8	16 43 11	17 12 38	10 51	9 36	2 39	5 50	22 54	8 32	2 51	8 02
9	17 40 23	29 52 18	11 19	9 59	3 11	6 02	22 56	8 32	2 50	8 01
10	18 37 35	12♈12 02	11 43	10 24	3 44	6 14	22 57	8 32	2 49	7 59
◐ 11	19 34 48	24 16 15	12 02	10 50	4 17	6 26	22 59	8 32	2 48	7 58
12	20 32 01	6♉09 58	12 16	11 18	4 50	6 38	23 00	8 32	2 47	7 56
13	21 29 15	17 58 21	12 26	11 47	5 23	6 50	23 02	8R32	2 46	7 55
14	22 26 29	29 46 25	12 32	12 18	5 56	7 02	23 04	8 32	2 45	7 53
15	23 23 44	11♊38 44	12R32	12 51	6 29	7 14	23 06	8 32	2 44	7 52
16	24 20 59	23 39 15	12 28	13 24	7 03	7 26	23 08	8 32	2 43	7 50
17	25 18 15	5♋51 06	12 19	13 59	7 37	7 37	23 10	8 32	2 42	7 49
18	26 15 32	18 16 25	12 05	14 35	8 11	7 49	23 12	8 32	2 40	7 48
● 19	27 12 48	0♌56 22	11 46	15 12	8 45	8 00	23 15	8 32	2 39	7 46
20	28 10 06	13 51 06	11 23	15 51	9 19	8 12	23 17	8 31	2 38	7 45
21	29 07 23	27 00 01	10 56	16 30	9 53	8 23	23 19	8 31	2 37	7 43
22	0♌04 41	10♍21 55	10 24	17 11	10 27	8 34	23 22	8 30	2 35	7 42
23	1 02 00	23 55 25	9 50	17 52	11 02	8 45	23 25	8 30	2 34	7 41
24	1 59 18	7♎39 14	9 12	18 35	11 37	8 56	23 27	8 29	2 33	7 39
25	2 56 38	21 32 20	8 31	19 19	12 11	9 07	23 30	8 29	2 31	7 38
◑ 26	3 53 57	5♏33 54	7 49	20 03	12 46	9 18	23 33	8 28	2 30	7 37
27	4 51 17	19 43 08	7 06	20 48	13 21	9 29	23 36	8 28	2 28	7 35
28	5 48 37	3♐58 55	6 22	21 34	13 57	9 40	23 39	8 27	2 27	7 34
29	6 45 58	18 19 18	5 39	22 21	14 32	9 50	23 43	8 26	2 26	7 33
30	7 43 20	2♑41 15	4 57	23 09	15 08	10 01	23 46	8 25	2 24	7 31
31	8 40 42	17 00 35	4 16	23 57	15 43	10 11	23 49	8 25	2 23	7 30

Day	Sidereal Time	True ☊	DECLINATIONS ☉	☽	☿	♀	♂	♃	♄	♅	♆	♇
	H M S	° ′	° ′	° ′	° ′	° ′	° ′	° ′	° ′	° ′	° ′	° ′
1	6:39:47	4R44	23N03	21S23	18N53	17N30	0N48	20N15	6S30	2N42	10S59	19S20
3	6:47:40	4♐40	22 54	20 20	18 03	17 25	0 21	20 20	6 31	2 42	10 59	19 20
5	6:55:33	4 29	22 43	14 07	17 15	17 23	0S06	20 25	6 32	2 43	11 00	19 21
7	7:03:26	4 17	22 30	5 10	16 28	17 24	0 34	20 29	6 33	2 43	11 01	19 21
9	7:11:19	4 09	22 16	4N14	15 44	17 26	1 02	20 33	6 35	2 43	11 01	19 22
11	7:19:12	4D07	22 00	12 30	15 05	17 31	1 30	20 37	6 36	2 43	11 02	19 22
13	7:27:05	4 09	21 43	18 34	14 30	17 38	1 58	20 41	6 38	2 43	11 03	19 23
15	7:34:58	4R10	21 25	21 31	14 01	17 45	2 26	20 45	6 40	2 43	11 04	19 23
17	7:42:52	4 04	21 04	20 36	13 38	17 54	2 54	20 49	6 42	2 43	11 05	19 23
19	7:50:45	3 50	20 43	15 46	13 23	18 04	3 23	20 53	6 44	2 43	11 06	19 24
21	7:58:38	3 31	20 20	7 45	13 15	18 14	3 52	20 56	6 46	2 42	11 07	19 24
23	8:06:31	3 16	19 56	1S58	13 16	18 25	4 21	21 00	6 49	2 42	11 08	19 25
25	8:14:24	3 08	19 30	11 32	13 25	18 36	4 50	21 03	6 51	2 41	11 09	19 25
27	8:22:17	3D08	19 03	18 48	13 41	18 47	5 19	21 06	6 54	2 41	11 10	19 26
29	8:30:10	3R08	18 35	21 36	14 04	18 57	5 48	21 09	6 57	2 40	11 11	19 26
31	8:38:03	2 59	18 05	18 51	14 32	19 08	6 17	21 12	6 59	2 39	11 12	19 27

Eris ⯰ July 1, 2012 22°♈41′52″ SR = July 19, 22°♈43′26″

Day	☉ ° ′ ″	☽ ° ′ ″	☿ ° ′	♀ ° ′	♂ ° ′	♃ ° ′	♄ ° ′	♅ ° ′	♆ ° ′	♇ ° ′
1	9♌38 05	1♒12 19	3R39	24♊47	16♎19	10♊21	23♎53	8R24	2R21	7R29
🌕 2	10 35 28	15 11 17	3♌05	25 37	16 55	10 31	23 56	8♈23	2♓20	7♑28
3	11 32 52	28 52 55	2 35	26 27	17 31	10 41	24 00	8 22	2 18	7 26
4	12 30 18	12♓14 06	2 09	27 19	18 07	10 51	24 04	8 21	2 17	7 25
5	13 27 44	25 13 29	1 50	28 10	18 43	11 01	24 07	8 20	2 15	7 24
6	14 25 12	7♈51 42	1 35	29 03	19 19	11 11	24 11	8 19	2 14	7 23
7	15 22 41	20 11 04	1 27	29 56	19 56	11 21	24 15	8 18	2 12	7 22
8	16 20 11	2♉15 21	1D26	0♋50	20 32	11 30	24 19	8 16	2 11	7 21
🌗 9	17 17 43	14 09 15	1 31	1 44	21 09	11 39	24 23	8 15	2 09	7 20
10	18 15 15	25 58 02	1 43	2 39	21 46	11 49	24 28	8 14	2 07	7 19
11	19 12 50	7♊47 10	2 02	3 34	22 23	11 58	24 32	8 13	2 06	7 18
12	20 10 26	19 41 58	2 28	4 30	23 00	12 07	24 36	8 11	2 04	7 17
13	21 08 03	1♋47 18	3 01	5 27	23 37	12 16	24 41	8 10	2 03	7 16
14	22 05 41	14 07 13	3 41	6 23	24 14	12 24	24 45	8 08	2 01	7 15
15	23 03 21	26 44 39	4 28	7 21	24 52	12 33	24 50	8 07	1 59	7 14
16	24 01 03	9♌41 05	5 21	8 18	25 29	12 42	24 54	8 05	1 58	7 13
🌑 17	24 58 45	22 56 24	6 21	9 16	26 07	12 50	24 59	8 04	1 56	7 12
18	25 56 29	6♍28 56	7 28	10 15	26 44	12 58	25 04	8 02	1 55	7 11
19	26 54 14	20 15 41	8 40	11 14	27 22	13 06	25 09	8 01	1 53	7 10
20	27 52 01	4♎12 58	9 58	12 13	28 00	13 14	25 13	7 59	1 51	7 09
21	28 49 49	18 16 57	11 22	13 13	28 38	13 22	25 18	7 57	1 50	7 08
22	29 47 37	2♏24 22	12 51	14 13	29 16	13 30	25 24	7 56	1 48	7 08
23	0♍45 27	16 32 44	14 25	15 13	29 55	13 37	25 29	7 54	1 46	7 07
🌓 24	1 43 19	0♐40 28	16 02	16 14	0♏33	13 45	25 34	7 52	1 45	7 06
25	2 41 11	14 46 33	17 44	17 15	1 11	13 52	25 39	7 50	1 43	7 05
26	3 39 05	28 50 06	19 29	18 17	1 50	13 59	25 44	7 48	1 41	7 05
27	4 37 00	12♑49 58	21 17	19 19	2 29	14 06	25 50	7 47	1 40	7 04
28	5 34 56	26 44 20	23 08	20 21	3 07	14 13	25 55	7 45	1 38	7 04
29	6 32 53	10♒30 44	25 00	21 23	3 46	14 19	26 01	7 43	1 37	7 03
30	7 30 52	24 06 15	26 54	22 26	4 25	14 26	26 06	7 41	1 35	7 02
🌕 31	8 28 53	7♓28 00	28 50	23 29	5 04	14 32	26 12	7 39	1 33	7 02

Day	Sidereal Time H M S	True ☊ ° ′	DECLINATIONS ☉ ° ′	☽ ° ′	☿ ° ′	♀ ° ′	♂ ° ′	♃ ° ′	♄ ° ′	♅ ° ′	♆ ° ′	♇ ° ′
1	8:42:00	2R51	17N50	15S41	14N47	19N13	6S31	21N14	7S01	2N39	11S12	19S27
3	8:49:53	2♐30	17 19	7 08	15 20	19 22	7 01	21 17	7 04	2 38	11 14	19 27
5	8:57:46	2 10	16 47	2N22	15 54	19 31	7 30	21 19	7 07	2 37	11 15	19 28
7	9:05:39	1 58	16 13	11 01	16 26	19 39	7 59	21 22	7 10	2 37	11 16	19 28
9	9:13:32	1D55	15 39	17 34	16 56	19 46	8 28	21 25	7 14	2 36	11 17	19 29
11	9:21:25	1R55	15 04	21 06	17 22	19 51	8 57	21 27	7 17	2 34	11 18	19 29
13	9:29:19	1 50	14 27	20 54	17 41	19 56	9 26	21 29	7 21	2 33	11 19	19 30
15	9:37:12	1 36	13 50	16 45	17 54	19 59	9 55	21 31	7 25	2 32	11 20	19 30
17	9:45:05	1 13	13 12	9 11	17 58	20 00	10 24	21 33	7 28	2 31	11 22	19 31
19	9:52:58	0 50	12 33	0S30	17 52	20 00	10 53	21 35	7 32	2 30	11 23	19 31
21	10:00:51	0 34	11 53	10 18	17 35	19 58	11 21	21 37	7 36	2 28	11 24	19 32
23	10:08:44	0D28	11 12	17 57	17 07	19 55	11 50	21 39	7 40	2 27	11 25	19 32
25	10:16:37	0R28	10 31	21 20	16 27	19 50	12 18	21 41	7 44	2 25	11 26	19 33
27	10:24:30	0 26	9 49	19 26	15 36	19 43	12 46	21 42	7 49	2 24	11 28	19 33
29	10:32:23	0♐07	9 06	13 03	14 35	19 34	13 14	21 44	7 53	2 22	11 29	19 33
31	10:40:17	29♏43	8 23	4 09	13 25	19 23	13 42	21 45	7 57	2 21	11 30	19 34

Eris ⯰ Aug. 1, 2012 22°♈42′28″℞

SEPTEMBER 2012 — Noon Greenwich Mean Time

Day	⊙	☽	☿	♀	♂	♃	♄	♅	♆	♇
1	9♍26′55″	20♓33′39″	0♍46	24♋32	5♏43	14♊38	26♎18	7R37	1R32	7R01
2	10 24 58	3♈21 55	2 43	25 36	6 23	14 44	26 23	7♈35	1♓30	7♑01
3	11 23 04	15 52 49	4 40	26 39	7 02	14 50	26 29	7 33	1 28	7 00
4	12 21 11	28 07 50	6 37	27 43	7 41	14 56	26 35	7 31	1 27	7 00
5	13 19 21	10♉09 45	8 34	28 48	8 21	15 01	26 41	7 28	1 25	7 00
6	14 17 32	22 02 25	10 30	29 52	9 01	15 07	26 47	7 26	1 24	6 59
7	15 15 45	3♊50 36	12 26	0♌57	9 40	15 12	26 53	7 24	1 22	6 59
◑ 8	16 14 01	15 39 30	14 21	2 02	10 20	15 17	26 59	7 22	1 20	6 59
9	17 12 18	27 34 37	16 15	3 08	11 00	15 22	27 05	7 20	1 19	6 58
10	18 10 37	9♋41 19	18 09	4 13	11 40	15 26	27 11	7 17	1 17	6 58
11	19 08 59	22 04 29	20 02	5 19	12 20	15 31	27 17	7 15	1 16	6 58
12	20 07 23	4♌48 04	21 53	6 25	13 01	15 35	27 23	7 13	1 14	6 58
13	21 05 48	17 54 33	23 44	7 31	13 41	15 39	27 30	7 11	1 13	6 57
14	22 04 16	1♍24 32	25 33	8 38	14 21	15 43	27 36	7 08	1 11	6 57
15	23 02 45	15 16 26	27 22	9 44	15 02	15 47	27 42	7 06	1 10	6 57
● 16	24 01 17	29 26 32	29 09	10 51	15 42	15 51	27 49	7 04	1 08	6 57
17	24 59 50	13♎49 27	0♎56	11 58	16 23	15 54	27 55	7 01	1 07	6 57
18	25 58 25	28 19 02	2 41	13 06	17 04	15 57	28 02	6 59	1 05	6D57
19	26 57 02	12♏49 19	4 26	14 13	17 45	16 01	28 08	6 57	1 04	6 57
20	27 55 41	27 15 21	6 09	15 21	18 26	16 03	28 15	6 54	1 02	6 57
21	28 54 21	11♐33 36	7 51	16 28	19 07	16 06	28 22	6 52	1 01	6 57
◐ 22	29 53 03	25 42 00	9 32	17 36	19 48	16 08	28 28	6 50	1 00	6 57
23	0♎51 47	9♑39 34	11 13	18 44	20 29	16 11	28 35	6 47	0 58	6 58
24	1 50 32	23 25 59	12 52	19 53	21 11	16 13	28 42	6 45	0 57	6 58
25	2 49 19	7♒01 04	14 30	21 01	21 52	16 15	28 48	6 42	0 55	6 58
26	3 48 08	20 24 36	16 08	22 10	22 33	16 16	28 55	6 40	0 54	6 58
27	4 46 58	3♓36 05	17 44	23 19	23 15	16 18	29 02	6 37	0 53	6 58
28	5 45 51	16 34 54	19 20	24 28	23 57	16 19	29 09	6 35	0 52	6 59
29	6 44 45	29 20 28	20 55	25 37	24 38	16 20	29 16	6 33	0 50	6 59
○ 30	7 43 41	11♈52 35	22 29	26 46	25 20	16 21	29 23	6 30	0 49	6 59

Day	Sidereal Time	True ☊	DECLINATIONS ⊙	☽	☿	♀	♂	♃	♄	♅	♆	♇
	H M S	° ′	° ′	° ′	° ′	° ′	° ′	° ′	° ′	° ′	° ′	° ′
1	10:44:13	29R31	8N02	0N34	12N47	19N16	13S56	21N46	7S59	2N20	11S31	19S34
3	10:52:06	29♏11	7 18	9 26	11 27	19 03	14 23	21 47	8 04	2 18	11 32	19 35
5	10:59:59	29 01	6 33	16 25	10 01	18 47	14 50	21 48	8 08	2 17	11 33	19 35
7	11:07:52	29D00	5 48	20 30	8 31	18 29	15 16	21 49	8 13	2 15	11 34	19 36
9	11:15:46	28R59	5 03	20 59	6 59	18 09	15 43	21 50	8 18	2 13	11 35	19 36
11	11:23:39	28 53	4 18	17 37	5 25	17 47	16 09	21 51	8 22	2 11	11 36	19 36
13	11:31:32	28 37	3 32	10 44	3 49	17 23	16 34	21 52	8 27	2 10	11 37	19 37
15	11:39:25	28 16	2 46	1 20	2 14	16 57	17 00	21 53	8 32	2 08	11 38	19 37
17	11:47:18	27 58	1 59	8S43	0 39	16 30	17 24	21 53	8 37	2 06	11 40	19 38
19	11:55:11	27 49	1 13	16 57	0S55	16 00	17 49	21 54	8 41	2 04	11 41	19 38
21	12:03:04	27D49	0 26	20 58	2 27	15 29	18 13	21 54	8 46	2 02	11 42	19 39
23	12:10:57	27R49	0S21	19 41	3 59	14 55	18 36	21 55	8 51	2 00	11 43	19 39
25	12:18:50	27 42	1 07	13 53	5 28	14 20	18 59	21 55	8 56	1 58	11 44	19 39
27	12:26:43	27 28	1 54	5 27	6 56	13 43	19 21	21 55	9 01	1 56	11 44	19 40
29	12:34:37	27 09	2 41	3N43	8 21	13 05	19 43	21 55	9 06	1 54	11 45	19 40

Eris ⯰ Sept. 1, 2012 22°♈33′29″℞

OCTOBER 2012 Noon Greenwich Mean Time

Day	☉	☽	☿	♀	♂	♃	♄	♅	♆	♇
	° ′ ″	° ′ ″	° ′	° ′	° ′	° ′	° ′	° ′	° ′	° ′
1	8♎42 39	24♈11 37	24♎02	27♌55	26♏02	16♊22	29♎30	6R28	0R48	7♑00
2	9 41 40	6♉18 42	25 34	29 05	26 44	16 22	29 36	6♈25	0♓47	7 00
3	10 40 42	18 15 53	27 05	0♍15	27 26	16 23	29 43	6 23	0 45	7 01
4	11 39 47	0♊06 04	28 36	1 24	28 08	16 23	29 50	6 21	0 44	7 01
5	12 38 54	11 52 59	0♏05	2 34	28 51	16R23	29 57	6 18	0 43	7 02
6	13 38 03	23 41 02	1 34	3 44	29 33	16 23	0♏05	6 16	0 42	7 02
7	14 37 15	5♋35 08	3 02	4 55	0♐15	16 22	0 12	6 13	0 41	7 03
◑ 8	15 36 29	17 40 26	4 29	6 05	0 58	16 21	0 19	6 11	0 40	7 03
9	16 35 45	0♌02 03	5 55	7 16	1 40	16 20	0 26	6 09	0 39	7 04
10	17 35 04	12 44 36	7 21	8 26	2 23	16 19	0 33	6 06	0 38	7 05
11	18 34 24	25 51 41	8 45	9 37	3 06	16 18	0 40	6 04	0 37	7 06
12	19 33 47	9♍25 18	10 09	10 48	3 48	16 17	0 47	6 02	0 36	7 06
13	20 33 13	23 25 13	11 31	11 59	4 31	16 15	0 54	5 59	0 35	7 07
14	21 32 40	7♎48 36	12 53	13 10	5 14	16 13	1 02	5 57	0 34	7 08
● 15	22 32 10	22 30 05	14 13	14 21	5 57	16 11	1 09	5 55	0 33	7 09
16	23 31 41	7♏22 24	15 33	15 33	6 41	16 08	1 16	5 52	0 32	7 09
17	24 31 15	22 17 22	16 51	16 44	7 24	16 06	1 23	5 50	0 32	7 10
18	25 30 51	7♐07 13	18 08	17 56	8 07	16 03	1 31	5 48	0 31	7 11
19	26 30 28	21 45 32	19 23	19 07	8 50	16 00	1 38	5 46	0 30	7 12
20	27 30 07	6♑07 52	20 38	20 19	9 34	15 57	1 45	5 43	0 29	7 13
21	28 29 48	20 11 50	21 50	21 31	10 17	15 54	1 52	5 41	0 29	7 14
◐ 22	29 29 31	3♒56 42	23 01	22 43	11 01	15 50	2 00	5 39	0 28	7 15
23	0♏29 15	17 23 00	24 10	23 55	11 45	15 47	2 07	5 37	0 27	7 16
24	1 29 00	0♓31 58	25 17	25 07	12 28	15 43	2 14	5 35	0 27	7 17
25	2 28 48	13 25 12	26 21	26 19	13 12	15 39	2 21	5 33	0 26	7 18
26	3 28 37	26 04 19	27 24	27 32	13 56	15 35	2 29	5 31	0 26	7 20
27	4 28 28	8♈30 55	28 23	28 44	14 40	15 30	2 36	5 29	0 25	7 21
28	5 28 21	20 46 27	29 19	29 57	15 24	15 26	2 43	5 27	0 25	7 22
○ 29	6 28 16	2♉52 26	0♐12	1♎09	16 08	15 21	2 50	5 25	0 24	7 23
30	7 28 12	14 50 27	1 01	2 22	16 52	15 16	2 58	5 23	0 24	7 24
31	8 28 11	26 42 22	1 46	3 35	17 36	15 11	3 05	5 21	0 23	7 26

Day	Sidereal Time	True ☊	DECLINATIONS ☉	☽	☿	♀	♂	♃	♄	♅	♆	♇
	H M S	° ′	° ′	° ′	° ′	° ′	° ′	° ′	° ′	° ′	° ′	° ′
1	12:42:30	26R54	3S27	11N58	9S44	12N25	20S04	21N55	9S11	1N53	11S46	19S41
3	12:50:23	26♏48	4 14	18 00	11 04	11 43	20 25	21 55	9 16	1 51	11 47	19 41
5	12:58:16	26D48	5 00	20 52	12 22	11 00	20 44	21 55	9 21	1 49	11 48	19 41
7	13:06:09	26 51	5 46	20 04	13 37	10 16	21 04	21 55	9 26	1 47	11 49	19 42
9	13:14:02	26R51	6 31	15 36	14 48	9 30	21 22	21 55	9 31	1 45	11 49	19 42
11	13:21:55	26 44	7 17	8 00	15 57	8 43	21 40	21 55	9 36	1 43	11 50	19 42
13	13:29:48	26 32	8 02	1S39	17 02	7 55	21 57	21 54	9 41	1 41	11 51	19 43
15	13:37:41	26 22	8 46	11 27	18 03	7 05	22 13	21 54	9 46	1 40	11 51	19 43
17	13:45:35	26 18	9 30	18 42	19 00	6 15	22 29	21 53	9 52	1 38	11 52	19 43
19	13:53:28	26D20	10 13	20 56	19 54	5 24	22 44	21 52	9 57	1 36	11 52	19 44
21	14:01:21	26 22	10 56	17 44	20 42	4 32	22 58	21 52	10 02	1 34	11 53	19 44
23	14:09:14	26R22	11 38	10 41	21 26	3 39	23 11	21 51	10 07	1 33	11 53	19 44
25	14:17:07	26 16	12 20	1 53	22 05	2 45	23 23	21 50	10 12	1 31	11 54	19 45
27	14:25:00	26 09	13 01	6N57	22 37	1 51	23 34	21 49	10 16	1 30	11 54	19 45
29	14:32:53	26 03	13 41	14 25	23 04	0 57	23 44	21 48	10 21	1 28	11 54	19 45
31	14:40:46	26D01	14 20	19 21	23 23	0 02	23 54	21 47	10 26	1 27	11 55	19 45

Eris ⯰ Oct. 1, 2012 22°♈18′04″℞

Day	☉	☽	☿	♀	♂	♃	♄	♅	♆	♇
1	9♏28 11	8Ⅱ30 24	2♐26	4♎48	18♐20	15R06	3♏12	5R19	0R23	7♑27
2	10 28 14	20 17 17	3 01	6 01	19 05	15Ⅱ00	3 19	5 17	0♓23	7 28
3	11 28 19	2♋06 13	3 31	7 14	19 49	14 55	3 26	5 15	0 23	7 30
4	12 28 25	14 00 56	3 53	8 27	20 34	14 49	3 34	5 14	0 22	7 31
5	13 28 34	26 05 37	4 09	9 40	21 18	14 43	3 41	5 12	0 22	7 32
6	14 28 45	8♌24 42	4 17	10 53	22 03	14 37	3 48	5 10	0 22	7 34
☾ 7	15 28 58	21 02 38	4R17	12 06	22 47	14 31	3 55	5 08	0 22	7 35
8	16 29 12	4♍03 27	4 07	13 20	23 32	14 24	4 02	5 07	0 22	7 37
9	17 29 27	17 30 16	3 49	14 33	24 17	14 18	4 10	5 05	0 22	7 38
10	18 29 48	1♎24 36	3 20	15 47	25 02	14 11	4 17	5 04	0 22	7 40
11	19 30 10	15 45 45	2 41	17 00	25 47	14 05	4 24	5 02	0D22	7 41
12	20 30 32	0♏30 15	1 52	18 14	26 32	13 58	4 31	5 01	0 22	7 43
✴ 13	21 30 56	15 31 56	0 54	19 27	27 17	13 51	4 38	4 59	0 22	7 44
14	22 31 22	0♐42 22	29♏48	20 41	28 02	13 44	4 45	4 58	0 22	7 46
15	23 31 50	15 52 02	28 34	21 55	28 47	13 36	4 52	4 56	0 22	7 48
16	24 32 20	0♑51 45	27 16	23 09	29 32	13 29	4 59	4 55	0 22	7 49
17	25 32 50	15 33 54	25 55	24 23	0♑18	13 22	5 06	4 54	0 22	7 51
18	26 33 22	29 53 22	24 35	25 37	1 03	13 14	5 13	4 52	0 22	7 53
19	27 33 56	13♒47 39	23 17	26 51	1 48	13 07	5 20	4 51	0 23	7 54
☾ 20	28 34 31	27 16 39	22 04	28 05	2 34	12 59	5 27	4 50	0 23	7 56
21	29 35 06	10♓22 04	20 59	29 19	3 19	12 51	5 34	4 49	0 23	7 58
22	0♐35 42	23 06 44	20 04	0♏33	4 05	12 43	5 40	4 48	0 24	8 00
23	1 36 20	5♈34 00	19 18	1 47	4 51	12 35	5 47	4 47	0 24	8 01
24	2 36 59	17 47 25	18 44	3 01	5 36	12 27	5 54	4 46	0 25	8 03
25	3 37 40	29 50 20	18 22	4 16	6 22	12 19	6 01	4 45	0 25	8 05
26	4 38 21	11♉45 47	18 11	5 30	7 08	12 11	6 07	4 44	0 26	8 07
27	5 39 04	23 36 28	18D12	6 44	7 54	12 03	6 14	4 43	0 26	8 09
☾ 28	6 39 48	5Ⅱ24 45	18 23	7 59	8 40	11 55	6 21	4 43	0 27	8 11
29	7 40 33	17 12 48	18 43	9 13	9 25	11 47	6 27	4 42	0 27	8 12
30	8 41 20	29 02 41	19 13	10 27	10 11	11 39	6 34	4 41	0 28	8 14

Day	Sidereal Time	True ☊					DECLINATIONS				
			☉	☽	☿	♀	♂	♃	♄	♅	♆	♇
1	14:44:43	26♏02	14S39	20N35	23S30	0S26	23S58	21N47	10S29	1N26	11S55	19S45
3	14:52:36	26 04	15 16	20 18	23 37	1 21	24 06	21 45	10 34	1 24	11 55	19 46
5	15:00:29	26 07	15 53	16 25	23 34	2 17	24 13	21 44	10 38	1 23	11 55	19 46
7	15:08:22	26R07	16 29	9 29	23 20	3 12	24 19	21 43	10 43	1 22	11 55	19 46
9	15:16:15	26 06	17 03	0 24	22 54	4 08	24 24	21 41	10 48	1 21	11 55	19 47
11	15:24:08	26 04	17 36	9S22	22 13	5 03	24 28	21 40	10 53	1 19	11 55	19 47
13	15:32:01	26 03	18 08	17 25	21 18	5 58	24 31	21 38	10 57	1 18	11 55	19 47
15	15:39:55	26D03	18 39	20 54	20 10	6 53	24 32	21 37	11 02	1 17	11 55	19 47
17	15:47:48	26 03	19 09	18 31	18 53	7 47	24 33	21 35	11 06	1 16	11 55	19 47
19	15:55:41	26R03	19 37	11 43	17 37	8 41	24 33	21 33	11 11	1 15	11 55	19 47
21	16:03:34	26D03	20 04	2 59	16 29	9 34	24 31	21 32	11 15	1 14	11 54	19 47
23	16:11:27	26 04	20 29	5N58	15 35	10 26	24 29	21 30	11 20	1 14	11 54	19 47
25	16:19:20	26 06	20 53	13 00	15 03	11 17	24 25	21 28	11 24	1 13	11 54	19 47
27	16:27:13	26 07	21 15	18 54	14 50	12 08	24 21	21 26	11 28	1 12	11 53	19 48
29	16:35:06	26R06	21 35	20 55	14 55	12 57	24 15	21 24	11 32	1 12	11 53	19 48

   Eris ♓ Nov. 1, 2012 21°♈59′43″R

Day	☉	☽	☿	♀	♂	♃	♄	♅	♆	♇
1	9♐42 08	10♋56 35	19♏50	11♏42	10♏57	11R31	6♏40	4R41	0♈29	8♑18
2	10 42 57	22 56 50	20 34	12 56	11 44	11♐23	6 47	4♈40	0 29	8 18
3	11 43 47	5♌06 06	21 24	14 11	12 30	11 14	6 53	4 39	0 30	8 20
4	12 44 39	17 27 23	22 20	15 26	13 16	11 06	7 00	4 39	0 31	8 22
5	13 45 32	0♍03 58	23 21	16 40	14 02	10 58	7 06	4 38	0 32	8 24
6	14 46 26	12 59 14	24 25	17 55	14 49	10 50	7 12	4 38	0 32	8 26
7	15 47 22	26 16 21	25 34	19 10	15 35	10 42	7 18	4 38	0 33	8 28
8	16 48 19	9♎57 47	26 45	20 24	16 21	10 34	7 25	4 37	0 34	8 30
9	17 49 17	24 04 42	27 59	21 39	17 07	10 26	7 31	4 37	0 35	8 32
10	18 50 16	8♏36 13	29 15	22 54	17 54	10 18	7 37	4 37	0 36	8 34
11	19 51 17	23 28 54	0♐33	24 09	18 40	10 10	7 43	4 37	0 37	8 36
12	20 52 19	8♐36 27	1 54	25 23	19 27	10 02	7 49	4 37	0 38	8 38
13	21 53 21	23 50 11	3 16	26 38	20 13	9 54	7 55	4 37	0 39	8 40
14	22 54 24	9♑00 05	4 39	27 53	21 00	9 46	8 01	4D37	0 40	8 42
15	23 55 28	23 56 20	6 03	29 08	21 47	9 38	8 06	4 37	0 41	8 44
16	24 56 32	8♒30 53	7 28	0♐23	22 33	9 31	8 12	4 37	0 43	8 46
17	25 57 37	22 38 46	8 54	1 38	23 20	9 23	8 18	4 37	0 44	8 48
18	26 58 42	6♓17 44	10 21	2 53	24 07	9 16	8 23	4 37	0 45	8 51
19	27 59 48	19 28 55	11 48	4 08	24 54	9 08	8 29	4 38	0 46	8 53
20	29 00 53	2♈14 12	13 16	5 23	25 40	9 01	8 34	4 38	0 48	8 55
21	0♑01 59	14 38 43	14 45	6 38	26 27	8 54	8 40	4 38	0 49	8 57
22	1 03 05	26 46 53	16 14	7 53	27 14	8 47	8 45	4 39	0 50	8 59
23	2 04 11	8♉43 32	17 43	9 08	28 01	8 40	8 51	4 39	0 52	9 01
24	3 05 18	20 33 15	19 13	10 23	28 48	8 33	8 56	4 40	0 53	9 03
25	4 06 25	2♊20 06	20 43	11 38	29 35	8 26	9 01	4 41	0 54	9 05
26	5 07 32	14 07 30	22 14	12 53	0♑22	8 20	9 06	4 41	0 56	9 07
27	6 08 39	25 58 14	23 45	14 08	1 09	8 13	9 11	4 42	0 57	9 10
28	7 09 46	7♋54 27	25 16	15 23	1 56	8 07	9 16	4 43	0 59	9 12
29	8 10 54	19 57 47	26 48	16 38	2 43	8 01	9 21	4 43	1 00	9 14
30	9 12 02	2♌09 31	28 20	17 53	3 30	7 55	9 26	4 44	1 02	9 16
31	10 13 10	14 30 49	29 52	19 08	4 17	7 49	9 30	4 45	1 03	9 18

Day	Sidereal Time	True Ω	DECLINATIONS									
	H M S		☉	☽	☿	♀	♂	♃	♄	♅	♆	♇
1	16:43:00	26R02	21S54	19N16	15S14	13S46	24S08	21N22	11S36	1N11	11S53	19S48
3	16:50:53	25♍58	22 11	14 12	15 44	14 32	24 00	21 20	11 40	1 11	11 52	19 48
5	16:58:46	25 54	22 27	6 31	16 23	15 18	23 51	21 18	11 44	1 11	11 51	19 48
7	17:06:39	25D54	22 41	2S42	17 06	16 02	23 41	21 16	11 48	1 11	11 50	19 48
9	17:14:32	25 56	22 53	10 58	17 51	16 44	23 30	21 14	11 52	1 10	11 50	19 48
11	17:22:25	25 59	23 03	18 52	18 38	17 25	23 17	21 12	11 55	1 10	11 49	19 48
13	17:30:18	25R56	23 11	20 50	19 25	18 04	23 04	21 10	11 59	1 10	11 49	19 48
15	17:38:11	25 49	23 18	16 56	20 10	18 41	22 50	21 08	12 02	1 11	11 48	19 48
17	17:46:04	25 41	23 22	9 01	20 53	19 16	22 34	21 06	12 06	1 11	11 47	19 48
19	17:53:58	25 36	23 25	0N14	21 33	19 49	22 18	21 05	12 09	1 11	11 46	19 48
21	18:01:51	25D37	23 26	8 56	22 10	20 19	22 00	21 03	12 12	1 11	11 45	19 48
23	18:09:44	25 40	23 25	15 12	22 43	20 48	21 42	21 01	12 15	1 12	11 44	19 48
25	18:17:37	25R41	23 22	20 02	23 12	21 14	21 22	20 59	12 18	1 12	11 43	19 48
27	18:25:30	25 35	23 18	20 45	23 37	21 37	21 00	20 58	12 21	1 13	11 42	19 47
29	18:33:23	25 24	23 11	17 48	23 57	21 58	20 40	20 56	12 24	1 14	11 41	19 47
31	18:41:16	25 04	23 03	11 38	24 12	22 16	20 20	20 55	12 26	1 14	11 40	19 47

Eris ♓ Dec. 1, 2012 21°♈44'54"Rx

	CERES ⚳		PALLAS ⚴		JUNO ⚵		VESTA ⚶		CHIRON ⚷	
	LONG.	DECL.	LONG.	DECL.	LONG.	DECL.	LONG.	DECL.	LONG.	DECL.
Jan. 1	24♓42	10S43	16≈30	02S24	22♏35	10S13	05♓06	14S57	01♓56	05S39
9	26 54	09 27	19 00	02 21	24 52	10 25	08 33	13 34	02 20	05 33
17	29 18	08 08	21 33	02 13	27 01	10 31	12 04	12 09	02 46	05 26
25	01♈50	06 48	24 09	02 00	29 02	10 32	15 39	10 42	03 14	05 17
Feb. 2	04 30	05 26	26 47	01 42	00♐52	10 27	19 16	09 12	03 44	05 08
10	07 16	04 03	29 26	01 21	02 32	10 17	22 56	07 42	04 15	04 58
18	10 09	02 40	02♓06	00 55	03 58	10 02	26 37	06 11	04 46	04 47
26	13 06	01 16	04 46	00 27	05 10	09 41	00♈20	04 40	05 18	04 36
Mar. 5	16 07	00N07	07 25	00N03	06 06	09 14	04 03	03 09	05 50	04 25
13	19 12	01 29	10 04	00 36	06 45	08 43	07 46	01 39	06 21	04 13
21	22 19	02 51	12 41	01 10	07 04	08 07	11 29	00 09	06 51	04 02
29	25 28	04 11	15 17	01 44	07♐03	07 28	15 12	01N18	07 20	03 51
Apr. 6	28 40	05 29	17 49	02 19	06 40	06 45	18 55	02 44	07 47	03 40
14	01♉52	06 46	20 19	02 53	05 56	06 01	22 36	04 07	08 12	03 29
22	05 06	08 00	22 45	03 26	04 52	05 16	26 16	05 27	08 35	03 20
30	08 19	09 11	25 07	03 58	03 30	04 33	29 55	06 45	08 54	03 11
May 8	11 33	10 20	27 23	04 27	01 54	03 53	03♉31	07 58	09 11	03 03
16	14 47	11 26	29 34	04 53	00 09	03 18	07 06	09 09	09 25	02 56
24	18 00	12 28	01♈37	05 16	28♏21	02 49	10 38	10 15	09 35	02 50
Jun. 1	21 11	13 27	03 33	05 34	26 37	02 29	14 07	11 16	09 42	02 46
9	24 22	14 22	05 20	05 46	25 01	02 17	17 33	12 14	09 45	02 42
17	27 30	15 13	06 57	05 52	23 39	02 15	20 56	13 06	09♈44	02 41
25	00♊36	16 00	08 21	05 51	22 36	02 21	24 14	13 54	09 40	02 40
July 3	03 40	16 44	09 33	05 41	21 52	02 36	27 28	14 37	09 32	02 41
11	06 40	17 23	10 29	05 22	21 28	02 58	00♊37	15 15	09 21	02 44
19	09 36	17 58	11 08	04 51	21D26	03 26	03 41	15 48	09 07	02 47
27	12 28	18 30	11 27	04 08	21 44	03 59	06 38	16 15	08 50	02 53
Aug. 4	15 14	18 58	11♈25	03 12	22 20	04 36	09 28	16 39	08 31	02 59
12	17 54	19 23	11 01	02 02	23 14	05 17	12 09	16 57	08 10	03 06
20	20 27	19 45	10 13	00 38	24 24	05 59	14 41	17 11	07 48	03 14
28	22 52	20 04	09 00	01S00	25 48	06 42	17 01	17 22	07 25	03 22
Sep. 5	25 07	20 20	07 26	02 50	27 25	07 26	19 09	17 28	07 02	03 31
13	27 11	20 36	05 33	04 48	29 13	08 10	21 03	17 32	06 39	03 41
21	29 01	20 50	03 26	06 51	01♐11	08 53	22 40	17 33	06 17	03 50
29	00♋37	21 05	01 13	08 52	03 19	09 34	23 58	17 32	05 58	03 59
Oct. 7	01 55	21 20	29♓02	10 47	05 35	10 14	24 54	17 30	05 40	04 07
15	02 54	21 37	27 01	12 31	07 57	10 51	25 27	17 28	05 25	04 14
23	03 31	21 56	25 17	14 00	10 26	11 25	25R33	17 26	05 13	04 21
31	03 44	22 18	23 55	15 12	13 01	11 57	25 11	17 25	05 05	04 27
Nov. 8	03R31	22 43	23 00	16 06	15 40	12 24	24 21	17 25	05 00	04 31
16	02 53	23 11	22 30	16 44	18 23	12 48	23 03	17 27	04D59	04 34
24	01 49	23 42	22D29	17 05	21 10	13 08	21 23	17 31	05 01	04 36
Dec. 2	00 23	24 14	22 52	17 13	24 00	13 23	19 25	17 37	05 08	04 37
10	28♊40	24 46	23 40	17 09	26 52	13 34	17 20	17 45	05 18	04 36
18	26 48	25 17	24 51	16 54	29 46	13 40	15 16	17 55	05 32	04 33
26	24 56	25 44	26 21	16 30	02♑41	13 42	13 23	18 07	05 49	04 30
28	24 29	25 51	26 46	16 22	03 25	13 41	12 58	18 11	05 54	04 28

Name

Place

Date   Time

Longitude   Latitude

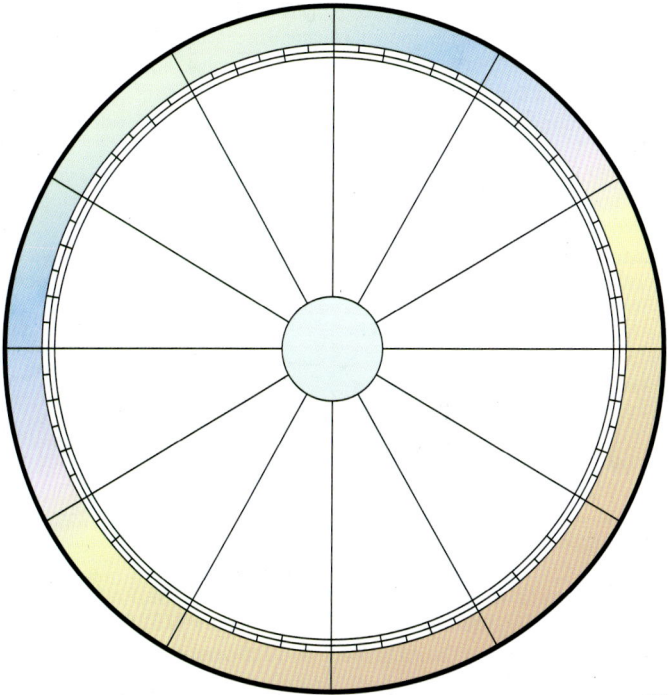

More Calendars

Pocket Astrologer® is also available as a full-color, 48-page wall calendar, **Celestial Influences**®, which unfolds to 12 x 18 inches. **Celestial Guide**® is a week-at-a-glance engagement calendar with either a plastic spiral binding or loose, 7-hole punched pages and includes an ephemeris and address book (176 pages, 5⅝ x 8½ inches, b&w illustrated). **Astrologer's Datebook**® is a bound, smaller-sized version of Celestial Guide at 4¼ x 6¾ inches.

Celestial Influences® **2012** wall calendar, Eastern or Pacific $12.95
Pocket Astrologer® **2012**, Eastern or Pacific $6.95
Celestial Guide® **2012** engagement calendar, plastic spiral bound $11.95
Celestial Guide® **2012** loose pages, 7-hole punched edition $11.95
Astrologer's Datebook® **2012** engagement calendar $8.95
The Handbook for Reading the Yearly Astrological Calendar $12.95

Prices effective through June 2012.

Order online at www.QuicksilverProductions.com using any charge card or send check or money order, including Shipping and Handling, to Quicksilver Productions or send information for Visa or MasterCard.

Discounts: For U.S. orders, subtract $1.00 if payment is made by check, cash, or money order. If the subtotal of the order is over $75 *before* adding Shipping & Handling, subtract 10%. If the subtotal of the order is over $150, subtract 15%.

Shipping & Handling Charges: Add Shipping & Handling charges as listed in this table based on the subtotal of the order.

For **foreign orders,** order online on our web site, or fax or email for shipping & handling charges.

Shipping & Handling: U.S. Insured		
Subtotal of order is ⮐	**First Class** or Priority‡	**Media Mail** *
up to $7.00	$3.50	$3.50
$7.01–$16.00	$7.00	$5.00
$16.01–$30.00	$9.00	$7.00
$30.01–$50.00	$11.00	$8.00
$50.01 and up	$13.00	$9.00

‡ First Class over 13 ounces becomes Priority Mail.
* Media Mail is much slower than First Class/Priority.

Send orders to: **Quicksilver Productions, Dept. PAK12**
P.O. Box 340, Ashland, Oregon 97520 U.S.A.
www.QuicksilverProductions.com
CelestialCalendars@email.com   541-482-5343 *fax: 508-590-0099*